A Tale of Two Cultures

A Tale of Two Cultures
A Personal Account

Ibrahim M. Oweiss

NEW ACADEMIA PUBLISHING VELLUM

Washington, DC

Library of Congress Control Number: 2011931923
ISBN 978-0-9836899-0-4 paperback (alk. paper)
ISBN 978-0-9836899-1-1 hardcover (alk. paper)

 An imprint of New Academia Publishing

 New Academia Publishing
PO Box 27420, Washington, DC 20038-7420
info@newacademia.com - www.newacademia.com

To my wife, Céline

To my daughter, Yasmeen and her husband, Mark Burns
To my son, Kareem and his wife, Julia Noble White
To my granddaughter, Ashling Burns
To my grandson, Kieran Joseph Burns
To my granddaughter Sofia White Oweiss

To the thousands of students I taught in the U.S. and elsewhere

and

To the most notable student. I take great pride for having taught him:
William Jefferson Clinton
42nd President of the United States

"Do unto life as though you live forever, and do unto your after life as though you die tomorrow."
—*Prophet Muhammad*

"Man fears time, yet time fears the Pyramids."
—*Arab proverb*

"From this day on, every drop of oil is worth a drop of blood."
—*Prime Minister of France Georges Clemenceau to President Woodrow Wilson*

"We live in a wonderful world that is full of beauty, charm and adventure. There is no end to the adventures that we can have if only we seek them with our eyes open."
—*Jawaharlal Nehru, Indian statesman*

Pride

After the heroic peaceful revolution of millions in Tahrir (Liberation) Square and all over Egypt from January 25 to February 11, 2011, to put an end to the corrupt, oppressive regime of Mubarak that lasted thirty years, I am proud to have been born in Egypt.

Here are some statements on this historic event:

President Barack Obama: "We must educate our children to become like young Egyptian people."

Britain's Prime Minister David Cameron: "We must consider teaching the Egyptian revolution in schools."

BBC: "Amazing, demonstrators line up at security checks, then enter the Square peacefully to make a revolution."

CNN: "For the first time, we see people make a revolution and then clean the streets afterwards."

Silvio Berlusconi, Prime Minister of Italy: "There is nothing new in Egypt. Egyptians are making history as usual."

Jens Stoltenberg, Prime Minister of Norway: "Today we are all Egyptians."

Austrian President Heinz Fischer: "The people of Egypt are the greatest people on earth; and they deserve the Nobel Prize for Peace."

J. William Middendorf II, Secretary of the Navy made this sketch during my address at the Committee for Monetary Research & Education (CMRE) at Arden House, Columbia University.

Contents

To Dr. Ibrahim Oweiss
With best wishes, & thanks   Bill Clinton

Preface

by President William Jefferson Clinton

When I entered Georgetown University's School of Foreign Service in 1964, I enrolled with the hope that I could learn a great deal about the world beyond the borders of my home state and nation. I wanted to understand how other people lived and thought, practiced their faiths, and raised their children. I wanted to learn about economics and politics and about how peace, freedom, and security could be achieved in these areas.

At the School of Foreign Service, I had the opportunity to learn from an extraordinary group of scholars whose knowledge and experience continue to influence me today. One of them was Ibrahim M. Oweiss, who taught my class in international economics and who later rose to prominence for his contributions in explaining the impact of oil pricing and revenues in world trade.

Professor Oweiss joined the Georgetown faculty in 1967, and I enrolled in one of the first classes he taught there. Drawing upon his experiences growing up in Egypt and as a young man studying for his Ph.D. in the United States, Professor Oweiss had a clear grasp of the intricacies of an increasingly global society, the economic impact of global trade in commodities like oil, and the economic benefits of free trade. He also shared his understanding of the Arab world and the root causes of the Arab-Israeli conflict. Professor Oweiss believed that our common humanity could triumph over our differences in his homeland. These lessons proved valuable years later, as I worked to broker peace in the region.

Oweiss held his position as a Professor of Economics on Georgetown's main campus for 35 years. While there, he wrote several important papers and participated in prestigious conferences on the economics of world trade and became a prominent lecturer, media commentator, consultant to multinational corporations, and advisor to world governments. He took a leave of absence from Georgetown in 1977 when President Anwar Sadat asked him to be the Chief of the Egyptian Economic Mission in the United States, to expand economic and commercial ties between our countries. When he returned to academia, he had increased his understanding of the world and his ability to provide his students with an invaluable combination of hard facts and personal reflections.

Three years after his initial retirement from Georgetown in 2002, the University asked for Professor Oweiss's assistance in establishing a branch of its School of Foreign Service in Qatar. Until 2009, he taught economics and helped to establish the Qatar program's character and identity, always taking an avid interest in developing both his students' intellects, and their hearts.

More than four decades have passed since I sat in Professor Oweiss's class. Like many of my fellow Hoyas, I have stayed in contact with him through the years. He brought his family to visit me in the Oval Office, and his daughter later volunteered her time during my Presidency as a White House intern. I also asked Professor Oweiss to join me for U.S.-Egypt summits and other diplomatic functions, and I remain indebted to him for sharing his insights with me while I was President and in the years since.

In his memoir *A Tale of Two Cultures*, he explores his life experiences in Egypt, the United States, and Qatar to capture these places, their people, and their traditions. A vivid storyteller, he creates a simultaneously intimate and intellectual narrative, putting his own experiences in the context of each culture's history. He describes the places he lived in and visited, the people he met, and the events he witnessed with detail and historical depth, which enable the reader experience the places, people, and events as he did.

In this engaging and charming personal narrative, Ibrahim Oweiss is once again the consummate teacher, the wise, generous, and dedicated professor and scholar of economics and geopolitics, with a real grasp of the complexities of human nature and society. He embodies the best values of the cultures that shaped him and also encourages his readers to embrace them to make the world a better place.

December 20, 2010

A Message

To my daughter Yasmeen, my son Kareem, and my students

Life starts with a cry, let it end with a smile
In your life, learn with joy and contribute from your heart
    While working to add a brick to human progress and prosperity.

If you succeed, be proud but not conceited
If you fail, be dignified but never despondent
    For success and failure are parts of human experience.

Read attentively what others write
And listen carefully to what others say
Even if their thoughts are different from your own
    For there ought not to be any monopoly over truth.

Never be an oppressor
    For think of yourself as being the oppressed
An oppressed suffers inhumanly during the ordeal, while
    An aggressor will someday die
    But the act of aggression remains forever
May we turn it into a remembrance in human consciousness
    So that it is not to be repeated.

Do remember that humans are created free
    With dignity and equality for women as well
    For today's woman is our future's mother.

Do learn that forgiveness emanates from strength
  While revenge is but a symptom of weakness
  For forgiveness and revenge exist in human consciousness.

If you lose your health, never lose your faith
If you lose your wealth, never lose your hope
If you deviate from success, never lose your drive.

Be strong and dignified
Be loving and caring.

Quoted and published in Mohamed Ali and Thomas Hauser, *Healing: A Journal of Tolerance and Understanding*, Collins Publishers, San Francisco, 1996.

Introduction

I meant to start my memoirs by reflecting on my experiences in contrasting one culture, that of Egypt where I was born and lived until the age of 28, with another, that of the United States where I have been deeply rooted in society since the day I landed in New York on March 7, 1960. For the title of the book, I thought of Charles Dickens's *A Tale of Two Cities*. But my life has encompassed much more than just Paris and London. It is, instead, a tale of two cultures.

I have always thought since long before I departed Egypt, the country of my birth, that Egypt is the past, Europe represents the present, and the United States is the future. Hence, I decided not to jump from the past to the future by taking an airplane from Cairo to the New World. It would neither have been fair to me nor to the make-up of my personality to be transplanted in the country of tomorrow after a few hours in the air. Instead, I decided to take *Esperia*, a Mediterranean ship, from Alexandria to Naples, to stay a few days in the great country of Italy. After my stay in Naples, I was booked on a huge transatlantic ship called *Saturnia* on my way to New York.

The thought came to my mind then: Now that I was in the New World, would I allow myself to be lost in its vastness or would I overcome, work hard, and compete in academia and in the other venues of life in the new, vast, and diversified world of incredible dimensions and wide horizons, a world of a scope I had never experienced before? I chose the latter.

A journey in academia followed. I taught at the University of Minnesota, Western Maryland College, Georgetown University, the School of Advanced International Studies (SAIS) of Johns Hopkins University, and Harvard University. Here, I recount the story of the new terminologies I contributed such as "petrodollars," "hostage capital," "the Oweiss demand curve," and "the Newton-Oweiss Law of social science." An elaboration follows of my involvement with many programs and activities in several countries and major international corporations as an advisor and an economic consultant.

A part of the book addresses the diversity of my civic activities and the institutional buildings where I worked, such as Georgetown University's Center for Contemporary Arab Studies, the Sultan Qaboos Faculty of Commerce and Economics in Oman, and others. My efforts as an activist for fairness and justice are to be accounted for. In addition I touch on my role in the many non-profit organizations I created, developed or otherwise participated in, as well as my experience serving President Anwar al-Sadat in 1977–78 as an ambassador and the Chief of the Egyptian Economic Mission to the United States headquartered in New York.

I served on the faculty of Georgetown University from September 1967 until my retirement in June 2002. Shortly after my retirement, I was elected to serve on the Georgetown University's Board of Regents. In 2005, I was asked if I was willing to join the pioneers who opened a branch of Georgetown University in Qatar. Without hesitation, I accepted. My experience in Qatar has been rewarding intellectually and educationally.

Throughout the book, I explain my political activism for human rights and fairness, and my opposition to the continuation of the Israeli occupation of the Arab land in violation of repeated United Nations Resolutions. I have always stood by the Palestinian and other people's inalienable rights for self-determination. In the same part, I illustrate my role in institutional building and civic affairs, be it in academia or non-profit organizations in the United States or elsewhere.

I am appreciative to the Georgetown University School of Foreign Affairs in Qatar for awarding me a Faculty Grant in two consecutive years. I also wish to thank Galal Aref, Thomas Gorguissian, Jessica Kane, Anna Lawton, Patricia O'Connor, Carole Sargent, and Joanne Smyth for having read an early draft and given me their valuable comments and editing. Technical support provided by Madelon Brennan and Sabry Latifi is much appreciated. Special thanks go to the editor, Paul Musgrave. Yet I am solely responsible about the contents of this book.

A Tale of Two Cultures

Foreword

The New Egyptian Pyramid

The events of early 2011 have raised a new pyramid in Egypt. Unlike the old pyramids, which were among the seven wonders of the ancient world, the new one was built in the hearts and souls of Egyptians wherever they are. It is an invisible pyramid representing their pride and dignity for having peacefully removed the tyrannical regime of Hosni Mubarak after thirty years of mismanagement, corruption, and deterioration in education, industry, agriculture, services, employment and the country's regional and international role.

It all started on January 25, 2011, which became known as the "Day of Revolt," when people in Cairo, Alexandria, Sinai, Suez, and other cities began to demonstrate peacefully in tens of thousands against the oppressive corrupt regime. I had just arrived in Qatar from the United Arab Emirates after having addressed the fourth World Energy Summit in Abu Dhabi on January 17, 2011. Headlines focused on the major historical revolt. As usual, Al-Jazeera was the first of the major television networks to cover the demonstrations. On Friday, January 28, peaceful protestors against Mubarak's regime started assembling shortly after Friday prayer in hundreds of thousands, camping around the clock. That day became known as the "Friday of Rage" in which people in Tahrir (Liberation) Square in Cairo and elsewhere demanded an end to corruption and the departure of Hosni Mubarak with banners flying everywhere—"NO HOSNI NOR HIS AIDES," "END THE THIRTY-YEAR OLD EMERGENCY LAWS," "WE LEAVE WHEN YOU LEAVE,"—some of which reflected the great Egyptian sense of humor: "DEPART MEANS LEAVE," "LEAVE, I MISS MY WIFE," and "DEPART, I AM TIRED OF CARRYING THIS BANNER".

The Nobel Laureate Mohammed ElBaradei traveled to Cairo to participate. He had been a vocal opponent of the Mubarak regime calling for peaceful transition to democracy and the rule of law. Amr Moussa, a former foreign minister of Egypt and Secretary General of the Arab League, whom I have known for the last forty years, was another famous personality who was spotted joining the demonstators in Tahrir Square. Both Mohammed ElBaradei and Amr Moussa have declared their candidacy for the presidency of Egypt.

The peaceful protests were the target of repression by the regime. On a sinister plan by Habib El Adly, the then Minister of the Interior in charge of the police and its security apparatus, prisons were opened and burned down, allowing inmates to escape to loot, commit crimes, harass the protesters, and terrorize the citizens so as to tarnish the reputation of the peaceful movement. The Egyptian government ordered the military to assist the police. International fear of violence grew, but no major casualties were reported. As slow as he has always been known to be, President Hosni Mubarak addressed the nation on January 28, 2011, for the first time after four days of protests by millions, including the central protests in Tahrir Square in Cairo. To pacify the growing movement, Mubarak asked Prime Minister Ahmed Nazif to hand in his resignation.

On January 29, protests continued as the military presence in Cairo increased. A curfew was instituted, but protests continued throughout the night. The military showed restraint, reportedly refusing to obey orders to use live ammunition; there were no reports of major casualties. The next day, after continued nationwide unrest, Mubarak addressed the people and offered several concessions. In addition to proclaiming that he would not run for another term in the September 2011 elections, he promised political reforms. He said that he would stay in office to ensure a peaceful transition. Undercover police and paid mercenaries carrying pro-Mubarak banners clashed with anti-Mubarak groups in small but violent interactions throughout the night. A group of demonstrators overpowered an undercover police, and pulled his ID card to show it clearly on television screens all over the world.

On the same day, I sent the following open letter to President Mubarak to newspapers in Egypt:

Your speech on February 1 was disappointing and alarming. With millions of Egyptians calling you to end your reign, you continue nevertheless to hold the office of the presidency against the will of the people. In addition to the great disappointment that you did not declare you are stepping down after thirty years of martial law, your defiance is alarming because it would lead to a deepening of instability, widening of demonstrations, disruption of life thus paralyzing the country, and further loss of life. *I urge you to step down.*

In the meanwhile, Mahmoud ElShazly, the president of the Egyptian-American Alliance headquartered in New Jersey, sent a circular of news coming from Egypt about a brave young Egyptian laid down before incoming army tanks. I sent an outcry to the President of the United States:

Dear Mr. President, I do appeal to you as an Egyptian-American who has been living in the United States for the last fifty-one years to interfere by all means to prevent a massacre similar to that of June 1989 on Tiananmen Square in Beijing in the People's Republic of China. As proud and determined young Egyptians are lining themselves today in Tahrir Square against slowly approaching tanks, I fear another Tiananmen crushing could be repeated nowadays in Cairo, Egypt.

The reply from the White House was assuring. I felt relieved when President Obama announced that it was time for Mubarak to go. In the meanwhile, the Egyptian Army commanders declared that the army would protect the Egyptian people allowing protestors to climb up the tanks and even show their banners calling for an end of Mubarak's regime.

On February 2, several camels and horses were unleashed into Tahrir Square following orders believed to be given by the Minister of Interior Habib El Adly, resulting in hundreds of casualties. Violence escalated as waves of Mubarak supporters in hundreds attacked the hundreds of thousands peaceful anti-government protestors. The military limited the violence, constantly separating anti-Mubarak and pro-Mubarak groups. President Mubarak, in interviews with various news agencies, refused to step down. Violence toward international journalists and news agencies escalated; speculation grew that Mubarak was actively increasing instability as a way to step in and end the protests.

Over the next several days, protests in Cairo and throughout the nation continued. Egyptian Christians held Sunday Mass in Tahrir Square, protected by a ring of Muslims. Negotiations began between Egyptian Vice President Omar Suleiman and opposition representatives. The Egyptian army increased its security role, maintaining order and protecting Egypt's museums. Suleiman offered political and constitutional reforms while other members of the Mubarak regime accused foreign countries, including the United States, of interfering in Egypt's affairs.

On February 10, Mubarak formally addressed Egypt amid reports of a possible military coup, but instead of his expected resignation, he stated his powers would transfer to Vice President Suleiman, and he would remain in Egypt as its head of state. Anger and disappointment spread through crowds in major cities all over Egypt, and demonstrations began to escalate in number and intensity throughout the country. The next day, the "Friday of Departure," massive protests in response to Mubarak's speech continued in many Egyptian cities. At 5:00 p.m. local time, Vice President Suleiman announced that Mubarak had decided to leave the presidency and that the Supreme Council of Egyptian Armed Forces would assume leadership of the country. Jubilant Egyptians celebrated the unbelievable event with outpouring emotions everywhere in the country and wherever they were in the diaspora. Tears, hugs, and singing where overwhelming. On the same evening, I was invited to the wedding of Samar Dayyoub, a Syrian physician practicing medicine in Qatar. At the table I was seated by prominent Syrians, Al-Mutaz Billah Al-Aidi, Ghazal Said, and Ghassan Murad, talking with utmost pride of what the Egyptians have achieved. Two days later, the Supreme Council of Egyptian Armed Forces dissolved Egypt's parliament and suspended the Constitution. The council also declared that it would hold power for six months or until elections could be held, whichever came first. ElBaradei urged the

Council to provide more details to the Egyptian people regarding its plans. Major protests subsided but uncertainty remained, and many pledged to keep returning to Tahrir square, while thousands were still camping, until all demands had been met.

On February 16, I attended a large rally of the Egyptian community working and living in Qatar along with other enthusiastic supporters in a football stadium. The world renowned clergy, Sheikh Yussef El-Qaradawi, addressed the large crowd among cheers and waving the Egyptian flags, while other banners were carried by happy crowds. Two days later, Yussef El-Qaradawi came from Qatar to address an estimated 2 million people in Tahrir Square with a moving sermon before the Friday prayer. It was a speech similar to the one he had given two days earlier in Doha.

I participated in the two-day Green Transportation Conference in Abu Dhabi on February 23 and 24, in an attempt to contribute to world understanding of the need to save carbon energy and to rely on other sources friendly to our environment. After the end of Mubarak's regime, I made my reservations to fly to Egypt for the first time in two years. I had avoided the country for years because of fear from the regime's prosecution following my published statements and television interviews about its corruption, adding my voice to others calling for ending it. Upon arrival at Cairo Airport on February 24, the official stamping my passport recognized me. I was relieved when he said, "Welcome back, Dr. Oweiss."

Events leading to the downfall of Mubarak's regime started to accumulate long before January 25, 2011. It included spread of poverty, unemployment, lack of housing, oppression by police force and State Security Investigation (SSI) headquartered in Alexandria, the continuation of Emergency Laws originally initiated when Mubarak took office in 1981, depriving people of their freedoms, exposing them to painful investigations and the use of torture ending with death or injuries, or psychological traumas. But the spark that ignited the Egyptian Revolution of January 25 was the torture of the 27-year-old Khaled Mohamed Saeed and the smashing of his face until death on June 6, 2010. He was caught by the notorious SSI in Sidi Gaber in Alexandria while he was at a cyber café fiddling with Facebook. In no time, photos of his disfigured corpse spread all over Egypt and even outside the country. In Washington, D.C., I was on my way to the Egyptian Embassy and saw a demonstration with banners carrying the face of Khaled Saeed. The least I could do was to join the demonstrators in utter disbelief of his torture until death by the Egyptian security forces. Wael Ghoneim moderated a Facebook page saying "We are all Khaled Said" with more than one and a half million subscribers. As it turned out, it was Facebook that led to a super organization of the Egyptian Revolution and the peaceful march calling for an end to Mubarak's regime and the emergency laws, and the dissolution of the Egyptian parliament. Another important straw that broke the camel's back was the irregularities in the last elections in Egypt on November 28, 2010, and the second round held on December 5, 2010. The National Democratic Party (NDP), the party of Mubarak, managed to marginalize the opposition, frighten out voters or bribe others. NDP won the vast majority of the parliamentary seats while the opposition was left out with 1.1% of the total seats. Observers and human rights groups concluded it was the most fraudulent election ever.

I went to Tahrir Square on February 25, 2011 where a couple of journalists recognized me and suggested that I speak before a large crowd of hundreds of thousands still camping there. From an elevated podium I spoke of the historic achievements of the young, resourceful Egyptians with admiration for their impeccable organization and their collaborative nature. I ended up by saying, "At this unique juncture in history, I propose that the new constitution would start with 'We, the people of Egypt.'" Upon repeating it, a thunderous sound from the largest enthusiastic crowd I have ever addressed kept echoing it in the Tahrir Square with jubilant cheers. I had never been moved in public in my entire life as I did in those moments. Although the full historical impact of the Egyptian revolution has yet to unfold, I know that it was one of the most significant moments of my life.

With the unbelievable success of the Egyptian revolution in ending Mubarak's regime, I believe that the priorities ahead necessitate first writing a draft for a new constitution by world renowned experts in constitutional law, in addition to the two Nobel laureates, Mohammed ElBaradei and Ahmed Zewail, as well as Boutros-Boutros Ghali, M. Cherif Bassiouni, Mansour Hassan, Saad Eddin Ibrahim, Naguib Sawaris, Bahie Eldin El-Ebrashi, Fayza

Aboulnaga, Ayman Nour and other well-known, highly qualified persons, and a cross section of individuals that can be nominated by the group of youth who energized and organized the people during their revolt, followed by approval through a national referendum. The draft may not be approved in the first round, but with modifications a final draft would eventually emerge no matter how long it takes, because a new constitution would be the strong base upon which a presidential election, followed by parliamentary elections, can be held. If the parliamentary or presidential elections are to be held before a new constitution is agreed upon, it would be as though a pyramid would be constructed upside down.

1

From the Deck of *Esperia*

The night before I left for the United States, I went in complete solitude to my family's salon, an ornate corner room in our villa where my family formally received our guests. Individual chairs along with two long central ones were placed against the four walls with the exception of a place for a beautifully designed glass door leading to a balcony that also served as a private entrance. On the glass door, two decorative see-through white drapes were hanging with hand-made lace peacock figures with long tails that spread down as if they were designed for a bridal dress. On the walls, my father had placed pictures showing his late father and uncle in nineteenth-century formal suits with starched high white collars, and his mother in a Turkish dress with many ruffles. There were other pictures of family members around those main ones in two rows. Two marble tables with golden rims sat on an oriental rug.

On the corner desk, I connected my tape recorder to a record player to leave a special message to each member of the family, with the soundtrack of one of my favorite pieces of music, "The Blue Danube" by Johann Strauss II. I asked that they listen to it after my departure. I was later told that my parents played it frequently as long as they lived. I started with a message of deep appreciation to my parents for all what they had done for all of us as a family and for me in particular. To augment his salary, my father had sold most of the land he inherited to provide us with an upper middle class standard of living. He bought luxuries for all of his children but absolutely nothing for himself. My mother was completely devoted to the service of her husband and her family. I remembered the sleepless nights as they both stood by my bed when I was hit by a high fever, giving me the medicine I needed and caressing my forehead with wet towels. For every brother and sister, I managed to collect childhood stories to relive such a memorable age with joy mixed with tears. I poured all of my 28-year-old emotions in a deep sober voice while recording, thinking that I might never see them again. Whenever I felt I was choking, I would raise the music volume until I was able to catch my breath before resuming recording. I wanted my family to listen to a confident voice reflecting hope for the future.

The next morning, I left for a world unknown to me.

I grew up in a tight-knit family, surrounded by the warmth and affection of our neighbors. Because of that upbringing in the internationally cosmopolitan city of Alexandria, with sizeable percentages of Greeks, Italians, Maltese, and others in addition to a multiplicity of mosques, churches and synagogues, I became a Renaissance man before I left Egypt. Alexandria is known sometimes as the pearl of the Mediterranean, or the sea's bride. Lawrence Durrell described it as "the capital city of Asiatic Europe, if such a thing could exist." I was proud to have spent most of my youth in the great city of Alexandria. Following the death of Alexander the Great, Ptolemy turned the city into the intellectual and cultural center of the world. It was estimated that the library of Alexandria before it was burned had more than half a million documents in several fields of knowledge. World-renowned scientists including Archimedes and Euclid lived and worked in Alexandria's ancient library.

I began my journey from Egypt to the United States on February 20, 1960, a crisp, sunny morning. Family members gathered at our villa to see me off. I hugged my mother, my four sisters, and my two sisters-in-law at our suburban villa in Victoria, Alexandria. Those who did not accompany me to the ship stood at our large northeast balcony bidding me farewell. I even felt that our garden Guava trees, from which we enjoyed eating delicious fruit, waved their branches to say good-bye.

My family's villa was surrounded by a garden on all sides. Our gardener took pride in adding greenery such as mint and arugula—a great addition to salad—and other small plants. On one side, the gardener planted tomatoes and had meticulously cared for the Guava trees that had their branches dangling on one part of our large north veranda and from which we could reach out to pick ripe fruit while in season.

To the west, the seventy-year-old Mr. Faber used to sit at his east balcony in full attire. His wife, who was probably even older than him, used to serve him a five o'clock tea with biscuits, cakes and chocolate. They were Jews and British subjects who came originally from Malta. Even if I were in a hurry, they would often insist I joined them for a cup of tea and conversation. Mr. Faber was an anti-Zionist. He thought that Jews like himself had been living in peace among Muslims and Christians in the Middle East for centuries while they were prosecuted in western predominantly Christian nations. But Zionism, a western ideology, separated the two peoples of Semitic origin, Arabs and Jews, the sons and daughters of Abraham. He often used to say that Zionism would always create wars and lead to destruction and instability in the lands of the three monotheistic religions. How prophetic he was. He showed me how he monitored his savings portfolio and how to choose stocks that seemed to be on the rise. Much of their investments were in the form of Suez Canal stocks. His outlook on life was full of wisdom that had enriched my own thinking for years and prepared me to understand the western mentality long before I left for the United States.

To the east, Madame Nina used to look from her western balcony to ask about family members. She was Greek, and her husband, El-Deeb Bey, was a prosperous broker in the cotton exchange market. While the Ottoman title "Effendi" was the equivalent to "mister," "Bey" and "Pasha"—the highest rank, equivalent to Lord—were bestowed by the King. Even though Nasser's revolution of 1952 abolished those titles, Egyptians still use them out of respect and a deep-rooted custom that can never change with any revolution. El-Deeb Bey and his Greek wife, Madame Nina, had one daughter living abroad. She visited her parents from Australia frequently. Her 12-year old son, Lorry, was the same age as my brother Zakaria, and the two used to play soccer with one another or laugh loudly at each other's jokes. Years later, my brother wrote me of her passing, which took place when he was in the last year of medical school. In great pain, she had crawled to the window and called for him. He heard her cries, jumped the fence, and ran to the door—but it was locked. He opened the window instead, and tried to give her first aid, but it was too late. She died in his arms before the ambulance he had called arrived.

I took a last look at my home and my neighborhood. I turned to the balcony of our villa where my mother, my sisters, and my sisters-in-law were standing waving with tears dropping on their faces while Madame Nina waved at me with lots of emotions and the Fabers held me for a few minutes, giving me last-minute advice as if I were the son they never had. Mrs. Mostafa Mohamed across the street kept waving with a handkerchief in each hand from her fifth floor balcony until I got in the car. My maternal uncle, Zaki Zeidan, a former member of Egypt's Parliament, insisted I ride in his green Mercedes on our way to Alexandria's main harbor. I sat holding my father's hand. Two of my uncles, Fouad and Abbas Zeidan, rode with us. My oldest brother Youssef and another brother Hassan rode in my brother Mohamed's car with my cousins Abdou and Khairy Zeidan and Saeed Shamseldin, who was engaged to my sister Khadiga. Ibrahim Fahmi, Saad Zaki, Hassan El-Khodeiri and many former students and friends followed in other cars.

As we turned to a busy main road only 25 yards from our villa, I looked east in the direction of the building of Nabila, my very first platonic love. Nabila was a beautiful girl three years younger than I. She had a round face with rosy cheeks and an attractive hairdo she managed to make like a flower on the left-hand upper corner just above her forehead. She had long hair that sometimes covered her charming deep brown eyes. I had first noticed her when I was 16 years old. She had come to spend a summer vacation in Alexandria. Her father worked in Hurgada, far away by the Red Sea. They stayed in an apartment where her aunt, the mother of Mahmoud Abdel-Meguid, a classmate of mine in high school, used to live. At first, we were too shy to look straight in each other's eyes. But we saw each other frequently enough to plant a seed in both of our hearts, something I often expressed in brief notes bundled with a small stone I would throw at her window. She reciprocated my poetry with her prose. A warm love feeling started to grow from afar without even meeting face to face. After her father died, her mother moved to Alexandria and rented an apartment on the first floor in the same building where my eldest brother Youssef had rented a unit on the second floor. Often, she would sneak out on the balcony so that we could touch hands. The touch made our hearts pump fast. My sister-in-law Gameela noticed the secret moments when Nabila and I talked and held hands while I was standing two feet below her balcony. When Gameela would notice from her bedroom window that I was coming, she would turn off all the lights and quietly go out on the balcony, just above that of Nabila.

Dating was not allowed at that time in Egypt. I dared to go to her uncle alone asking to marry her. He was rude. He utterly refused my proposal because I had not yet graduated. Unlike the other western cultures I became exposed to, marriage was to be arranged by the family. The father or whoever is the eldest in the girl's family had to affix his authoritative stamp of approval. Otherwise no marriage would take place, regardless of how the young couple felt towards one another.

For years, when I was living elsewhere in Egypt, whenever I returned to Alexandria I would pass by her balcony and we would hold hands and talk secretly. She knew I was leaving for the United States but neither of us knew when I would leave. When I looked towards her balcony, blood rushed throughout my veins as I saw her tears running down her beautiful face while she waved rather discreetly. She must have stood on her balcony for hours so as not to miss a last glance at me. I could not wave back as my father and uncles were completely in the dark regarding my secret love. Thank God traffic stopped because of a passing train. That gave us a few minutes to look passionately at each other. I must have poured into my gaze all the emotions of the most sacred expression of platonic love that gathered over eleven years. The train passed, and our car moved out of sight. We have not seen each other ever since.

From home, we drove north for a short while on what was known El-Siouf Street just before the Victoria College buildings, then we turned left heading west on what was known as Abou Keir Avenue, which was renamed El-Horreya Avenue after the 1952 revolution. I was filling my eyes with everything I saw. Memories crossed my mind as I saw the superb villas on both sides of the wide boulevard. On the right side was the famous Sporting Club with lots of greenery and trees. There I had attended the tennis world championship and watched Jaroslav Drobny, the left-handed world-famous player from Czechoslovakia, defeat Gottfried von Cramm, the aristocratic German who used to play in his long ultra-white trousers. Opposite the Sporting Club stood beautiful, tall residential buildings whose balconies were decorated with roses, pansies, begonias, greenery and other flowers.

Farther along, I could see the Faculty of Engineering, part of Alexandria University with its impressive façade with high pharaohonic columns resembling those of the Karnak Temple. As we entered downtown Alexandria, I asked my uncle if we could move a bit slower to look at the breathtaking view. The city was beautiful with its fountains and its stadium on the left of a green park surrounded by tall trees. The car moved forward to the historical Fouad Street with the well-designed buildings of the Governorship of Alexandria, the Greco-Roman museum and Mohamed Ali Theater. I turned my head to the right at Sisostris Street to have a last look at the office of my brother Mohamed at number 13. At the northwest corner of Sherif and Sisostris streets, I used to stop often for a drink at the well-known Brazilian coffee shop. I also saw one of the ornamented horse buggies, a *hantour*, with its owner sitting on a high elevated chair on top of the two front, well-polished brass lamps on both sides of the carriage. It was standing at the entrance of number 13 as if it were waiting for my brother. Mohamed used to leave his car in front of the building but, for short distances, he loved to take those horse buggies. Because of his generous tips and his friendly gestures, he was known and favored by their owners.

We kept moving on Sherif Pasha Street. We passed the Bourse, the stock market of Alexandria. La Bourse of Alexandria was well known and connected in trade with stock exchanges in New York, London, Zurich, New Orleans and others. For cotton transactions, it was posted with the Chicago Board of Trade and other commodity trading centers around the world. The cosmopolitanism of Alexandria was in full evidence at the street corners around La Bourse. There, you could hear people speaking in Arabic, English, French, and other languages at the same time. Leaving La Bourse behind, we entered the grand square of Mohamed Ali Pasha, the founder of modern Egypt and the founder of the dynasty that ended with Nasser's revolution in 1952. There stood a statue of him on horseback, wearing an Albanian turban.

We proceeded to the western harbor of Alexandria. As we got out of the cars, I started to hug first my father, then my uncles, my brothers, other members of the family and all those who came to bid me farewell. I boarded the ship *Esperia*, a Mediterranean ship with a regular route between Alexandria and Naples. My older brother Mohamed had a successful export-import business and he knew the ship's captain and pursers. He had given me a ticket for passage from Alexandria to New York and a heavy camel hair coat he knew I would need in the cold weather of Minnesota, where I would live for a few years. The bill I still have from Adriatica, the company that owned *Esperia*, showed the total price for a third class ticket from Alexandria to Naples of 24.535 Egyptian pounds, the equivalent of $61.37 or about $429 today. With a handsome tip, my brother Mohamed was able to get me an upgrade to a first-class cabin, while asking the captain to arrange for the same favor once I boarded *Saturnia* for the voyage from Naples to New York. My generous brother had also paid $215 for a third class ticket on *Saturnia* from Naples to New York (the equivalent of 86 Egyptian pounds in 1960, about $1,540 today).

My luggage was carried to my cabin while I climbed up a rickety gangplank. I was holding to the ship's rail with one hand, while waving an handkerchief with the other to my family on the pier. At 5:00 p.m., the ship's loud horn started to blow and the gangplank was gradually lifted by strong ropes. In a few minutes, a steamboat pulled the ship slowly out of its location. The distance between the ship and the pier kept widening, but we were still waving to one another, and could still hear the loudest good-bye shouts.

My family became smaller and smaller until we could no longer see each other, but I found myself still waving with both hands, holding a handkerchief in each. As we left the harbor, I kept looking at Alexandria from afar, seeing all her white buildings floating on a dish of water. They became ever smaller as we sailed off until we sank gradually in the horizon seeing only the tip of tall buildings until they completely disappeared leaving room for an infinite blue sky all around us. As the city disappeared, I kept thinking of spots I used to go to along its coastline, such as dancing in the dim lights of Pergola, enjoying pastries at shops such as Delices, Pastroudis, Boudrot, Sofianopoulo Coffee Shop and numerous others, and watching movies at Cinema La Getée in a Greek district in Al-Ibrahimya. And so I recalled my childhood in Egypt.

My parents married very young. My mother delivered eighteen children but eight died in infancy. My first sister, Zeinab, was born in 1934, the second, Khadiga, was born in 1936, the third, Aicha, was born in 1937, the fourth, Fatma, was born in 1942 and my last living brother, Zakaria, was born in 1944. Zeinab lives in Alexandria and Eicha lives in Cairo while Khadiga, Fatma, Zakaria and I live with our families in the United States. Zakaria is an obstetrician/gynecologist immigrated to the United States, where he had a private practice in Washington, D.C., and was affiliated with Washington Hospital Center, Columbia Hospital for Women, Georgetown Washington Hospital, and Sibley Hospital. Those who died in infancy were Imam, Ibrahim, Yehia, Hassan, Ahmed, Nefeesa, Hussein and Zakaria. On three cases, my father used the same name of a deceased infant for a newborn baby. Hence, there was another "Ibrahim" who died in infancy before I was born.

With so many children, my father thought it would be more comfortable for my mother to have the babies delivered by a midwife at the spacious home of my mother's family, some fifty miles southeast of Alexandria, in a town called Abou-el-Matamir. At that time, even in the United States, most babies were born at home with the assistance of midwives. My mother's brothers were well to do. Three brothers were engaged in business and trade and others were involved in politics. My uncle Zaki was a member of the Egyptian parliament in his district, Abou-el-Matamir in the province of Behaira, after having won the election several times. My mother's family had a four-story building, each floor consisting of two apartments facing one another. The entire building was only for the family. I was born there on September 25, 1931.

My father was of Turkish origin and used to have his moustache well trimmed and waxed with one pointed shape sticking upward on each of the two sides. He was bilingual in both Arabic and English. When I started to be aware of my surroundings in the mid-1930s, I used to observe him going to work across the street from where we lived. He was the headmaster of Victoria railroad station. Often, he used to wear his formal attire called Redding

Coat, the equivalent to a white tail, with impeccably polished shoes covered by attractive fitted suede. That was the time when Farouk, the newly inaugurated King of Egypt, was scheduled to pass by in his royal well-ornamented train with golden rails and handles. My father used to stand along with his staff on the platform to greet the King while passing through. In all the years he did such trips, the King never stopped at Victoria Station, or at any other station, he went from departing point which was a special station inside Montaza Palace to the east of Alexandria to the place of final destination.

I grew up in a typical patriarchal society. With the exception of the allocation and spending of his monthly salary that he left to my mother, my father was the obvious decision maker in all matters of our lives. The only person he listened to was my mother, in private. She had enormous power from behind the scenes. He had the greatest respect for her as a wife and a mother. He never called her in an authoritative voice, but he got her attention by saying tenderly, "*Sitt Hanem*," meaning, "the mother lady." We all loved him but were terrified if one of us did not behave. He instructed us, "If any of you did something wrong to any other, do not respond but write your complaint on a piece of paper and drop it in the mailbox." He was the one who had the key. Any quarrel would soon be settled amongst us and the youngest would be carried on the shoulders of the eldest in an attempt to fish the complaint out of the mailbox with the small fingers. If it did not work, the most able from us would stand on a chair dangling a pair of scissors to get the complaint out before my father would arrive. Alas, if the mailman had already collected the mail or if the scissors were to drop inside the mailbox!

When I was nine, I used to cross the street from where we lived to take the train in a comfortable twenty-minute ride from Victoria Station to the end of the line to go to school. I attended a primary school called Al-Attarin next to the main Alexandria railroad station, a huge well-decorated terminal for all trains coming to Alexandria. I thought at that time that it must have been the largest in the world, until I realized later that in fact it was relatively small, especially after I saw the Cairo railroad station. Later in life, of course, I saw even bigger ones, like London's Waterloo Station, New York

City's Grand Central Station, the Hauptbahnhof in Berlin, and the grand stations in Paris. Everything is relative.

When my schoolmates and I got out of the station, we walked up the northern ramp leading us to the level of the street going east to the stadium and west to a district called Attarin. By simply crossing the street at that point, we found ourselves facing our school's gate. Because of a strong pre-schooling education, I was placed in the second-year level in 1940. One of my classmates was Richard Afifi, who was called Dick. His mother was British and his father, Abou-el Ela Afifi, was a prominent professor of philosophy at King Farouk First University, later renamed Alexandria University after Nasser's 1952 revolution. Mr. Abdel-Aleem, our teacher, set an excellent example to us in cleanliness and how to be careful of one's own appearance and behavior. His suit was always well ironed, and in the morning he used to call on Dick and me to check if any of the pupils had potatoes in their ears. What he meant was to check if the students' ears were well cleaned. If they were not, Dick or I would just say, "potatoes." The pupil would be given a warning. If he still had dirty ears the next day, the school's nurse would check well on the following day. On the back of every notebook distributed to us, there were statements of advice such as "Do not postpone today's work until tomorrow," "Never promise what you cannot do," "Be disciplined and clean," "Straighten up your own faults before you attempt to straighten up those of others." Those statements were to be followed and to be adhered to. I have tried to do so ever since.

In 1942, the Germans under the command of Erwin Rommel, the "desert fox," having been successful in their battlegrounds in North Africa, reached El-Alamein some 70 miles from Alexandria. The city was bombarded heavily one night by planes aiming at British military targets. Several homes were destroyed. Bodies of killed or injured civilians were pulled out from the debris the following day. The city witnessed an exodus as never before, by cars, wagons, bicycles, motorcycles, trains and even on foot. The Egyptian government issued an order that civilians could get free rides on any means of transportation out of Alexandria. We were packed along with many others in a train compartment that usually took six people, on the leather chairs, on the floor and even on the luggage racks. Many who could not get inside the train climbed up on its roof where some of them were killed or injured from falling off or being hit by low bridges under which the train passed.

My mother held the six of us around her in one seat, while my father stood until we reached Kafr-el-Dawar, about 20 miles away. Soon after the train started to move slowly out of Sidi Gaber Station overlooking a combination of buildings and agricultural fields, a woman standing in the long corridor not far from our compartment screamed loudly while trying to open a window to throw herself out. I learnt that she had mistakenly wrapped a pillow in a blanket instead of her baby. She was prevented by other passengers, but was seen walking back in a hurry towards Alexandria when the train first stopped. In Kafr-el-Dawar, we pulled ourselves out of the train, amidst a large crowd, to take another railroad called Delta. It was a small train running on narrow tracks in a semi circle for about 50 miles, connecting several towns in the province of El-Beheira and going through towns such as Hosh Issa, Abou-el-Matamir and others. We had to be away for a few months until it was safe to re-turn to Alexandria, after Field Marshal Bernard Law Montgomery and the Allied forces defeated the Axis armies led by Field Marshal Erwin Rommel at El-Alamein. It was a turning point in the war.

Abou-el-Matamir was a small town with a ribbon of agricul-tural land to the west, and a vast western desert extending all the way to the Libyan border. While living there, I was treated as a Bey by the peasants who worked about 500 acres of land that my mater-nal uncles owned. They would rush to my assistance if I fell while playing with other children. I remember those days clearly. During my stay in Abou-el-Matamir and noticing the farmers' standard of living, I was amazed at the difference between urban and rural ar-eas. Once, I was given a donkey ride while a farmer was walking alongside me to protect me from falling. A few yards ahead of us, I noticed a woman staggering while walking. All of a sudden, I saw her going down a ditch behind a bush next to a running stream. I stopped to see if we could be of help to her. Soon we heard the scream of a baby. The farmer told me she had just delivered a baby. She cut the umbilical cord, wrapped and held the child in her arm, got out of the ditch and kept walking. I shall never forget the scene.

A memorable occasion arose by sheer chance. Just before finish-

ing junior high education at Ramleh Secondary School, King Abdul-Aziz Al-Saoud came for a state visit to Egypt in 1945. While in
Alexandria, the most respected and beloved philanthropist Prince
Omar Tousson, whose mansion was within walking distance from
our school, invited the Saudi King for a 5 o'clock tea. The Chief
of the Prince's Protocol office, Tashrifati, upon the orders from the
Prince himself, met with our headmaster Galal Yakout Bey to have
young students lined up on the pavement just outside the main
entrance of our Zervodaki building gardens and behind the color-
fully-dressed royal guards standing on the street at a hundred-yard
distance from one another. Several Royal motorcycles came in advance of the motorcade. We saw an open-hooded Rolls Royce in the
typical unique maroon color distinguishing royal cars from all others rolling before our eyes with windows widely opened. Amongst
our cheers, we saw the Saudi King Abdul-Aziz, who lost one eye
when he conquered the western province of Najd, in 1925. He uni-
fied the largest portions of the Arabian Peninsula and established
the Kingdom of Saudi Arabia in 1932, which turned out later on to
have been endowed with the largest deposits of oil in the world.

We could not believe how many children he had in his company, two were in each of the royal maroon-colored cars, one after
the other as if there was no end to it. Some were probably as old
as my father, including Prince Saud who became a king after the
death of his father in 1953, and Faisal, who later on became a king
from 1964 to 1975, while others were my age, such as Prince Nawwaf and Prince Meshari, both of whom I got to know in the journey
of life. In fact, Prince Mohamed, currently the Saudi ambassador to
the United Kingdom, the son of Prince Nawwaf, became a student
of mine at Georgetown University. Egyptians loved Prince Tousson
for his good deeds. Most conclude that if he had been the king of
Egypt in 1952 Nasser's revolution would not have occurred. But the
hands of the clock of history can never be reversed.

Upon graduation from primary school in 1943 in Alexandria, I
went to Ramleh secondary school not far away from home. As I had
always been thin and frail, I could not bear the physical efforts in
playing sports. Instead, I channeled my energies to reading. During
the high school years, I read and memorized lots of poetry in three
languages, Arabic, English and French. The essays I used to write

in class were oftentimes read aloud by my teachers. I read as many of the classics as I was able to lay my hands on. I was fascinated by great Arabic, English, and French authors as well as the translations of other giant Russian, German, and Spanish writers. My first piece of poetry was published when I was thirteen.

I had also become a public speaker as an activist against the British occupation of Egypt after I read about the national leaders of Egypt's modern history, Abdullah an-Nadim, Mostafa Kamel and Saad Zaghloul. I was only 10 years old when the whole country was terribly shocked by Sir Miles Lampson, the then British ambassador in Cairo. On February 4, 1942, he drove a British tank through the gates of Abdeen Palace in Cairo to deliver a threatening note well-engraved in my memory ever since: "If I am not to be informed by six o'clock this evening that Nahhas Pasha is asked to head the cabinet, King Farouk will bear the consequences." It was a flagrant violation against an independent state.

Even though Egypt gained its independence from the British in 1922 after a long national struggle under such notable figures as Abdullah An-Nadim, Mostafa Kamel, Saad Zaghloul, Mostafa El-Nahhas, Isamil Sedky, and Aly Maher, to name but a few, their troops and bases were deployed in strategic parts of the country and hence the powers of the British ambassador were overwhelming. He was a de facto ruler of Egypt from behind the scenes.

Resentment for the presence of the British army in Egypt was felt everywhere. The British had no reason to stay in the country after the end of World War II. Prime Minister Isamil Sedky Pasha flew to London to reach an agreement for British withdrawal in 1946. Word got around of unacceptable terms of what was known as Sedky-Bevin treaty. Demonstrations were mounted everywhere. I was fourteen, still very frail and thin yet with a strong voice. I was carried on the shoulders of other students to give a fiery speech. One of those attending this event was my colleague Hassan El-Abbadi, who later became Egyptian ambassador. His father, Abdel-Hamid El-Abbadi Bey, was a prominent intellectual and the dean of the Faculty of Literature at King Farouk First University. His brother, Mostafa El-Abbadi, a well-known historian, an authority on the history of the ancient Library of Alexandria, was also with us at school.

When I moved from Minnesota to Washington, D.C., in 1967, I went to renew my passport at the all-but-deserted Egyptian Embassy. Diplomatic relations between Egypt and the United States were severed following the 1967 war. To my delight and surprise, the head of Egypt's Interests Section then was Hassan El-Abbadi. He reminded me of the speech I gave at the demonstrations of 1946 at Ramleh Secondary School. When he said, "An Egyptian revolution can be put off by a spit," I replied, "Do not let the description of Lord Cromer apply to you. But let them now say, an Egyptian revolution cannot be extinguished even by an atomic bomb."

After my speech, we all went outside, filled the tramway composed of two wagons, and carried our banners, shouting and demanding an immediate evacuation of the British troops from the lands of Egypt. At the western end of the tramway station, police were waiting for us. They shoved us in trucks and took us to a temporary detention facility at the police station. It was a huge room with small windows twenty feet high so that no one could reach them. Fortunately, it was not long. Our headmaster, Galal Yakout, who carried the prestigious title of a Bey, came to the police station and got all of us released. That evening, my father gave me a piece of his mind, but seemed to have been proud of my early involvement and leadership as some of his words revealed.

Upon graduating from high school in 1948 at sixteen, I entered the Faculty of Commerce of King Farouk First University. It was temporarily located in a well-ornamented mansion in Laurent Alexandria until the construction of the university building would be completed in two years. It was about ten minutes by tramway from the beginning of the line from Victoria to Laurent. The tramway ran parallel to the fence of Victoria College at the eastern end of the line. There was a small kiosk rented by a fat Greek called Mandas with red big cheeks selling cigarettes, the Cadbury chocolate I loved, and other small items.

As in all of our educational systems in Egypt, at college we were properly dressed in suits and with neckties. The only difference was that I used to wear a red *tarboushe*, also known as a fez, when I was in the primary school. In the courtyard, a large wooden lecture hall was constructed. On the three-floor building, other upper classes were held while the main floor hosted the office of the Dean,

Shafeek Hassan Bey. The administration offices were located in an adjacent building. There was a narrow courtyard but sufficient for the small number of students at that time. Our dean held the position of Egypt's cultural attaché in London in the 1930s. He was tall, thin and impressive. His wife was British and his manners were those of a European more than an Egyptian. Several outstanding professors taught us. They were all American- or European-educated with Ph.D. degrees earned from prestigious universities such as Harvard, Oxford, the London School of Economics, and others.

I was not only enthusiastic about learning from great scholars and being involved in current affairs, be it in Egypt, the Middle East, or elsewhere, I became the chief editor of the College annual book and I wrote and published poetry and a magazine called *Risalat El-Shabab,* meaning *Youth Message.* It was in 1951 that a famous literary giant in the Arab world by the name of Taha Husayn visited the University after his appointment as the Minister of Education. On that occasion, I was assigned by our Dean, Shafik Hassan Bey, to prepare and read one of my poems.

Before the event, I was asked to meet Gohar Taha Pasha, the President of King Farouk First University, at his headquarters in Boulkly. King Farouk First University's Administration building was a mansion with a superb garden going uphill to the offices. As I was going up the wide white marble staircase to the second floor, I was thinking of what I ought to say to the University's President, whom I had never met before but who was familiar to me from the published pictures I saw. The appointment was at 11:00 am. I arrived at the office of his secretary a few minutes early. The well-dressed secretary was busy with some paperwork at his desk. He stood up, looked at the big mirror hanging on the wall, combed his hair and buttoned his jacket before he looked into an oval window placed on each side of a swinging door with green velvet cover.

He ushered me in. "You are two minutes late," the Pasha said. The words I thought of saying evaporated from my mind. I did not want to tell him that I arrived early and that his secretary was busy. As soon as I apologized, he looked at me with a sort of kindness I had not seen when I first entered. "Look my son, being exactly on time is a sign of respect for the person you meet. Consider this to be a life lesson you never forget," he said.

He continued. "Your dean admires your poetic talent. Can you read a good poem you composed or verses you can write in honor of the Minister of Education, Taha Husayn Pasha? Because he is blind, you should avoid using such words as 'see', 'look', or the like. He is extremely sensitive and would immediately figure out what you are doing if you avoid such words."

That was another lesson I learned for the rest of my life: treat the blind or the handicapped normally so that they do not feel any different from others. It was exactly 11:13, as the big watch behind his chair showed. He stood up, shook my hands and told me, "Thank you for coming and thank you for agreeing to greet the Minister with a poem. Good luck. I'll see you at the lecture hall at Littoria at the time, date and place shown clearly on the paper my secretary will give you as you leave." I saw a gentleman I did not recognize as a celebrity waiting at the secretary's office. I deduced that he must be the following appointment at 11:15.

The lessons I learned from the university's president were alien to an Egyptian way of life. Gohar Pasha adhered to and practiced the western lifestyle in every way: the way he was dressed, the manner of his speaking, the straightforwardness of his remarks, and the respect he showed to all others regardless of their social status.

Taha Husayn was called the Dean of Arabic Literature. He lost his eyesight at age three, when an infection he contracted was not properly treated. In spite of his handicap, he was a brilliant student throughout his education, be it Egypt or in France. He turned into a world-known philosopher and thinker. His literary critical evaluation of written works or plays he attended contributed to the fame he deserved. His compatriots had always admired his deep voice and the clarity of his mind. He was also known to express his thoughts with a simplicity that was impossible to imitate. In fact, President Anwar al-Sadat used to speak in Taha Husayn's style. In his book *A History of The Arab People*, the Oxford scholar Albert Hourani described him as the most original Arab writer.

The day had come to read my poem before Taha Husayn and other well-known dignitaries at Littoria. It was the building that had the Faculty of Law. At its northern side there was a large swimming pool where my high school classmate, Abdellatif Abou Heif, used to practice swimming for about two hours every day, another hour would be spent at the zoo watching how the dolphins swim.

He became a champion, breaking a world record in swimming across the British Channel from Calais in France to Dover in the United Kingdom. He also won the longest swimming distance at Lake Michigan in the United States. I accompanied him a few times to keep time of his laps. In that area there were also several tennis courts for faculty and students and a running track.

At Littoria's Lecture Hall, I was ushered to the stage three steps higher than the floor. I was very thin, but my voice was deep and strong. I brushed off the fear that came unto me and started reading my poem about Alexandria. After I finished, Taha Husayn asked to talk with me. It was an awesome moment. In spite of an inner trembling I walked steadily to where he was seated in the middle of the front raw, with the Governor of Alexandria on his right and Gohar Pasha to his left. Taha Husayn stood up touching my shoulders and chest; he then shook my hands saying, "Exactly as I imagined you to be: frail and not tall." He was known to be miraculously observant without eyesight. Voices and sounds formed an inside imagery in his mind. Suzanne, the French lady he met and married while studying in France during World War I, was his "eyes," love, and companion for life.

The year I entered the university coincided with the first Arab-Israeli war. Under the mentorship of our reputable historian Rashed El-Barrawi, Tahseen Basheer, who later on became Egyptian ambassador to Canada, and I formed a Society for Middle Eastern Affairs to study different aspects of this conflict. Tahseen was six years older than I and was a junior at that time. His brother Tayseer was among the first officers to die in the 1948 war. Our first meeting was held at a nearby resort called Beaurivage only two hundred yards from our College. Its quiet surroundings and beauty attracted top members of the society. I used to go there to read a book while enjoying tea with pastries or refreshing ice cream or else with a date, hiding in a corner as dating was not permitted at that time.

It was at the Beaurivage that I started my activism for what I believed to be a fair cause. During the university's two years at the temporary campus, the Society for Middle Eastern Affairs met occasionally in a room of this beautiful quiet resort. After we moved to the permanent campus in El-Shatby, our society met in one of the seminar rooms in my junior and senior years.

While I was at the university, I joined a program leading to Officers in Reserve, a program similar to ROTC in the United States. In Egypt, military service is obligatory except for certain cases as unfitness, being a sole son, being a brother of someone killed while being in the military service, or else, in the past, making a payment in lieu of service or obtaining a college degree. Every morning before lectures started we would spend one hour of military training, and for two months in the summer, for three consecutive summers, we attended a military camp on a full-time basis at the Military Academy or elsewhere. Upon completion, a university graduate would have the rank of second lieutenant in different branches of the army. I completed the program, and was called from my civilian work to have active military service twice before my departure from Egypt when my rank became captain. From 1954 to 1957, I was the commander of the National Guard at the Faculty of Commerce.

In June 1952, at the age of 20, I graduated from the Faculty of Commerce, at King Farouk First University, majoring in Economics and Political Science. The Egyptian government put a freeze on jobs right after the revolution unless there was a dire need for certain positions just as I graduated. Fortunately, an opportunity arose in August 1952. An advertisement appeared in major newspapers indicating that there was a need for French language teachers. Any college degree was accepted to fill any of the positions of French teachers in high schools provided that the applicant passed written and oral exams in the French language. I applied, took the exams and got my first job at Zagazig High School, some 150 miles away from home. My first monthly salary was fifteen Egyptian pounds, equal to $75 at the time or $1,420 today.

Zagazig High School was located by an irrigation canal in the capital of the Province of Sharkia, meaning Eastern Province, as it was located east of the Damietta branch of the Nile River. It was an immense building on about ten acres of land including its sports fields. I was twenty years old when I met my first class. To my surprise, I found several students older than me. In fact, a couple of them were married. At the beginning, they thought they could play high-school tricks on me, but it did not take long before I was able to set my rules of conduct straight and gain their respect. I played ping-pong with those students who were on the school's team and sat with others in the shade of tall trees in the school's courtyard to discuss current events or family matters.

I spent two years teaching there, commuting every weekend to Alexandria. It took almost three hours of travel each way, and so I applied for a transfer to a high school in my home town. I was soon pleasantly surprised that I was to be transferred to teach at Rashid High School, only twenty miles away from Alexandria. Rashid was a quiet small town known for its dates, farm produce and Nile sardines. It was also known to Egyptologists around the world as the place where the Rosetta Stone was discovered by French soldiers in 1799 at the time of the Napoleonic invasion of Egypt.

On the first day of class, one boy thought he could taunt me. He did not want to listen to what I had to say, but instead from time to time, he would come up with ugly revolting whistles making others holding down their laughs. As he refused to be disciplined, I insisted and finally succeeded to kick him out of the class. From my second floor window, I soon glimpsed a huge man with a big cane in his hand entering the school accompanied by the student I had just kicked out of class and another man carrying a big basket. I was scared and became even more frightened when I heard a knock on the door. I went to the other side of the class, while saying in a loud voice "open up." The man was too big to enter from one side of the door. Before he said anything, I asked him to meet me after class at the headmaster's office. One boy told me the student I had kicked out came from a big clan and that his father was the town's mayor.

When the bell rang ending the class session, several students walked behind me keeping some distance from me. I went down the staircase and entered the Headmaster's large office. The big man stood up and asked me pointing at the boy if I had kicked this pupil out of class and actually hurt his feelings. When I answered in the positive, he came to me, hugged me and said that I was the only teacher who dared to discipline his son. With the cane he was holding, he started hitting his son until the headmaster and I intervened to stop him. He shook hands with me and asked me if I needed anything in his town. He took what the other man was carrying, a basket full of red dates and guava, and gave it to me saying that it was a token of thanks.

"Where do you live?" he asked.

"In Alexandria," I replied.

"Do you have a car or do you take public transportation?" he asked. When he found out that I intended to take a bus, he insisted for having his car with the gifts wait for me outside after school to take me to our villa in Alexandria. It was an experience that I never forgot as I kept it always in my mind with all of its minute details.

I stayed only one month at the new location before I was called for duty as a first lieutenant in Egypt's National Guard and was posted at the very same college I graduated from two years earlier to train students in early morning classes. I was the post commander with two well-trained corporals as my staff. Every college formed a unit, called *Katiba*, of approximately 90 volunteers. North of Littoria in Shatby there was a large fenced area for all of the six Katibas to form a regiment once a month. It was the headquarters of the University National Guard with its military hierarchy and high-ranking officers. Faculty of Commerce unit was Katiba number 3. One of the students trained in my unit, Sultan Abou Ali, ranked high in the division of economics at Alexandria University's College of Commerce. He won a government scholarship to earn a Ph.D. in economics from Harvard University. Fifteen years after he returned to Egypt, he became the country's Minister of Economy. While studying at Harvard, he married Hanaa Kheir-el-Din, who was also studying economics at Massachusetts Institute of Technology (MIT) under the supervision of Robert Solow, a Nobel Prize winner.

On October 29, 1956, Israel, the United Kingdom, and France mounted their tripartite aggression against Egypt a few months after Nasser's nationalization of the Suez Canal. As soon as the war started, I was asked to be the commander of a National Guard at Fort KaitBey, at the northern tip of Alexandria. In a hurry, I moved my Katiba to the location with a full plan to defend the fortress against invaders

The war soon ended. In order to avoid an unnecessary conflict with the Soviet Union, which moved some of its naval ships in the Mediterranean, President Eisenhower ordered England, France and Israel to completely withdraw from Egyptian occupied territories.

During the summer time, the National Guard had a training

camp by the seashore at Al-Max west of Alexandria. In 1958, orders were issued for all camp volunteers to wear a national villager costume called *gallabiah* or *koftan*. Mount trucks were confiscated for the occasion from civilian drivers, and headed for Cairo to cheer President Nasser in a rally called "popular support for the unification with Syria." I refused to be part of that political charade. The commander of the camp, a general, summoned me to his tent and said, "Since you had been kind enough to explain to my daughter the course of statistics she had the most difficulty with, I have decided not to court martial you for refusing the high orders I received from Cairo. Instead, I'll give you a medical excuse for one week."

At that time, the closest medical hospital was in a part of Ras-el-Tin Palace transformed into an army medical center. As I was growing up, it never dawned on me in my wildest dreams that one day I would sleep inside any royal palace. Ras-el-Tin Palace was overlooking Alexandria's harbor. In fact, the King's yacht *Al-Mahrousa* used to have a special pier at the palace. It was from that palace that King Farouk departed for exile on *Al-Mahrousa* on July 26, 1952. The rooms were very spacious with a ceiling no less than thirty feet high and a large crystal chandelier hanging from the middle of the well-carved ceiling. From the room, with its own superb full bathroom, there was a large terrace where I used to sit and look at ships from afar, to read, or to sip tea, or drink a cold glass of lemonade.

My military duty ended in 1958. A former professor of mine arranged for my transfer from the Ministry of Education to the Ministry of Industry. He was a deputy minister working closely with his Minister, Dr. Aziz Sedky, who later on became prime minister. I was appointed the Director of Economic Evaluation of Industrial Projects reporting directly to the Deputy Minister. At meetings headed by the Deputy Minister, we had to study every proposed industrial project based on cost-benefit analysis. We also attempted to diversify industrialization in as much as was feasible. What we failed in was avoiding concentrations of industries in Cairo and in Alexandria. Shortly before my departure from Egypt, I presented a study to the Deputy Minister warning against such concentrations. The report created a problem for me as it was interpreted as though I was critical of Nasser's regime, which was dangerous. I used all my skills and connections to remove such a stain so that I could leave the country in peace.

Since I was almost finished with my studies for my Masters degree at Alexandria University, I thought of getting both a Masters and Ph.D. in the United States. I applied to Harvard University, Princeton University and the University of Minnesota. I decided to accept the first to reply. Even though I was admitted to all the three institutions, the first reply came from the University of Minnesota. And so it was that after six months of cutting through the notorious red tape of the Egyptian bureaucracy I would find myself on the deck of the *Esperia*.

At last, I was called away from my reveries by a bell ringing for dinner. My room was beautifully furnished with its own full bath. Through a small round window, I could see water and other floating vessels of different sizes and shapes. The steward whom my brother Mohamed had tipped handsomely told me that I was to be seated at the ship's restaurant with a beautiful *bambina* three years younger than me named Maria. She came from a wealthy family from Florence and had recently earned a master's degree in arts. She was fascinated by Egyptian history, and so as a graduation gift her family gave her a first-class ticket and a tour of Egypt's priceless antiquities. The food was delicious and the company was pleasant even though I did not understand Italian. Through her broken French and even worse English, we managed to communicate by drawing pictures or else through hand waving. We joked, we laughed, and we danced at music played by a superb band sometimes until past midnight. Whenever Maria saw me thinking of my family and the country I had left behind, she would not leave me alone until I cheered up.

We had an elaborate farewell dinner the night before we arrived in Italy. Tables were nicely decorated with ribbons to blow and balloons to throw to one another. Maria told me about her fiancé, a young physician, and about how the works of the art masters intoxicated her. When she learned I was planning to go to Rome, she advised me to visit Galleria Borghese to look at the works of Raphael, Bernini, Canova, and others. Maria had drunk too much champagne, and so I had to support her from time to time to keep her on her feet. Instead of retiring for the night, she insisted to dance and dance until she fell on the floor. I had no other alterative but to carry her to her cabin while she was singing and saying, "the night is still young!"—an English phrase she knew well.

The next morning, we disembarked in Naples. "There is my father!" she shouted joyfully. He was an impeccably dressed gentleman in his late forties with dark, well-groomed hair carrying a bouquet of red roses. Next to him was her fiancé Antonio. He was not at all handsome but rather short with a noticeable belly. Maybe she was attracted to him because of other characteristics, I thought. After all, they had come in a large Mercedes. I kissed her goodbye, and continued to Rome.

The architecture of the Italian capital impressed me immensely with its elegance, beauty, and functionality. The well-polished white marble and other colors of granite stones were everywhere. The buildings I entered were spotless as if they had just been meticulously cleaned. I vowed to myself that I would return to that city to spend there more than just a couple of days. As it turned out, Rome later became a stopping station in between my flights to and from the Middle East. I visited the Vatican, where I saw not only the beautiful Basilica of St. Peter but also the remarkable Pope John XXIII, who preached peace on earth and whose legendary approach to other religions gave him prominence in the history of the church. Churchmen in brightly colored costumes carried out the 79-year-old pontiff in a beautifully decorated palanquin. I was in the first row. I stretched my hand out to him while everyone else was applauding. He barely touched my fingers, but people around me rushed in my direction and put my hand on their faces and on their children. It was a moving scene that has been carved in my memory forever.

Following Maria's advice, my first stop was at Galleria Borghese where I stood breathless before Bernini's sculptures. The museum itself is a piece of art even before entering, with its two wings connected on the second floor by a majestic balcony while the center is recessed in the back for even higher floors. Stairs from both sides lead to a spacious welcoming entrance under a high oval arch from the top. For symmetry, there are two high oval arches on each side of the central entrance. The museum's curator explained that three schools (stressing human beauty, strength, and normal features) are shown in superb sculptures and in magnificent paintings such as Bernini's "David, Apollo and Daphne," "Pluto and Proserpina," and "Truth Unveiled by Time" in addition to Canova's sculpture of "Pauline Bonaparte" and that of Raphael's "The Deposition."

I soon had to leave Rome for Naples for the next leg of my travels. During the train ride, I was engulfed in deep thought about my first encounter with the western world. Even though I had formed ideas about it through my readings, movies and meeting the many Europeans who lived and worked in Alexandria, there was still much to learn. It became clearer to me than ever before that we Egyptians taught ancient Greeks and the Romans who in turn taught the Arabs. The Arabs built on those foundations, and having made major contributions to philosophy, medicine, astronomy, mathematics, and many other fields of knowledge, taught the Europeans and pulled them out from the dark ages into enlightenment.

In 1954, six years before I left Egypt, I saw a famous American movie, *Three Coins in the Fountain*, starring Clifton Webb and Dorothy McGuire. I saw it several times and had memorized its words. I asked the driver to go to the famous Trevi Fountain to see the romantic place where the film was shot. As I stood in front of it, listening to the sound of falling waters, I made a wish and tossed a few coins, while the song I memorized over the years kept repeating silently but joyfully in my mind.

Three coins in the fountain
Each one seeking happiness
Thrown by three hopeful lovers
Which one will the fountain bless?

Three hearts in the fountain
Each heart longing for its home
There they lie in the fountain
Somewhere in the heart of Rome
Which one will the fountain bless?
Which one will the fountain bless?

Three coins in the fountain
Through the ripples how they shine
Just one wish will be granted
Make it mine! Make it mine! Make it mine!

Upon arriving at my hostel in Naples, I was pleasantly surprised to see Maria waiting for me. She jumped in my arms with
tears of joy running on her apple-like cheeks. She said, "My father
has a business office here in Naples. I convinced him to stay for a
few days until you sail to New York. He has a commitment this
evening and left me the car with the chauffeur."

"Where is Antonio?" I asked.

"He had to fly back to be with one of his patients while she delivered her baby," she said. "He was sure that her due date was a
couple of days ago."

Maria's warm affection towards me was overwhelming. She
suggested that we go to a restaurant famous for its seafood. From
its rich ambience, I grew worried. I had a limited amount of money
I could take out of Egypt because of the country's strict money exchange controls initiated by Nasser's regime. Egypt's Central Bank
authorized only a meager amount of $100 to be taken out of Egypt,
an amount that was affixed to my Egyptian passport. And although
I had been able to obtain an equal amount of dollars on the black
market, I did not have any other means such as credit cards or a
checkbook. Through our close and intimate relationship all the way
from Alexandria to Naples, Maria knew what was on my mind. She
told me that she would pay for everything.

As we sat down, she confessed that she was now torn between
her love to her fiancé and her feelings towards me, whom she called
her young pharaoh. She thought that I added a rich dimension to
her life throughout the three-day cruise between Alexandria and
Naples. The food and drinks were outstanding while music in the
background was soft. She said, "Life is a sequence of moments. Let
us make every minute until we part to be an unforgettable time
of happiness that may hopefully compensate for any future mis-
ery." As we left the restaurant, the chauffeur knew exactly what her
plans were. He drove us to a nightclub. She danced and drank as if
there was no tomorrow to follow.

The following morning, Maria insisted to take me in her car

to the harbor all the way to the foot of the ship. It was difficult for both of us to say good-bye. Her tears were mixed with mine running warm on our faces as we were hugging one another. The ship's horn gave its passengers the signal to climb up the gangplank. We had to pull ourselves from one another. I walked slowly up the gangplank having my eyes fixed on her all the while. The ship pulled out of the harbor as we were waving until she faded out of sight. That was the last time I saw Maria.

Onboard, I was surprised to discover that the purser that my brother Mohamed had tipped handsomely in Alexandria so that he could upgrade my accommodations had in fact pocketed all the money for himself. I was alarmed to see that I would be sleeping in a bunker bed near the engines in a large common space full of poor immigrants from Italy. I asked to talk to the main purser. A tip I gave him made all the difference. I was assigned a nice cabin instead.

Onboard, we received world news from *Corriere Del Mare*, a two-page newspaper printed at sea based on radio news reports. I kept the issue of March 3, 1960. A sampling of its news is below:

Salem, Oregon. The names of six Democrats including Adlai Stevenson and two Republicans, including New York Governor Nelson Rockefeller, were entered for Oregon's May 20 presidential primary.

Chicago. President Eisenhower may keynote the Republican National Convention July 25, officials said.

Frankfurt, Germany. Well-wishers gathered at the airport today to cheer and shout good-bye to Elvis. More than one hundred Air Force and German police were on guard. Presley's 18 month tour with the U.S. Army in Europe came to an end when he stepped on board a military air transport plane.

Detroit. The Detroit Red Wings strengthened their grip on a NHL playoff position with a 3 to 2 victory over the Boston Bruins.

Kabul. Soviet Premier Nikita Khrushchev with an escort of Afghan MiG-17 fighter planes landed on a tour of Asian nations.

It was a different world in those days as I sailed across the Atlantic.

We had a few days of turbulence. On the eve of February 29, we were informed about an incoming storm and were advised to strap ourselves even in bed. The wind was ferocious with silver lightening appearing in the veins of otherwise dark skies. The floating city we boarded in Naples was tossed around by gigantic waves such as I had never seen before. The waves I was familiar with were rolling in white foam layers after layers. In the ocean, water dips in a valley as if the ship was just about to touch the ocean's bottom while waves on both sides were rapidly climbing higher than our vessel that seemed to have been reduced to no more than a child's toy. Some waves were rolling from high towards our vessel as if they were going to swallow the whole little thing in no time. We witnessed a rise of the body of waters carrying our ship from a valley to the tip of a high mountain while the waves that enclaved us subsided as deep skiing slopes. The skillful captain managed to direct the ship across the rising and falling bodies of waters rather than being at the mercy of their ups and downs. At times, the ship would be climbing at 45-degree angle then descending at an even greater angle. Most passengers became sick and fearful of sinking. Ropes in blue deep velvet were fastened between strong poles with a shining brass ball at the tip of each one. Tables, chairs and all other moving objects were tightly and securely chained. The passengers' reactions varied greatly. Some kept praying, some held their heads between their hands, a few looked aimlessly up, down or sideways, others could not control grinding their teeth, and some were screaming or crying but could not be heard in the midst of the roaring thunders. The crew was quick in tossing buckets of water to clean the ever increasing vomit of those who were unable to control themselves or did not have on them the proper anti sea-sickness medication. When the storm was finally over, *Saturnia* continued to sail smoothly. There were only rare days when the weather was calm. I saw not far from us a group of large whales dipping and rising again with their fountains going high up in the air and their smoothly-curved gigantic bodies just surfacing before diving again, leaving their wide tales gradually going last down in the water.

* * *

On March 7, 1960, I got up shortly after dawn so I could see the

Statue of Liberty as we approached the shores of the United States. I had no idea how colossal the Statue of Liberty was until I started seeing it in reality. As a symbol of liberty, the statue had a profound echo in my heart and mind throughout my life. Ever since I became aware of colonization in many parts of the world, I turned out to be active in defending liberation movements in my writings and in my public speeches.

I was informed I had officially arrived in the United States. When my two suitcases were unloaded, an inspector at the customs asked me if I had any vegetable or fruit that I was bringing from abroad. Upon informing him and showing him a package of Amar-eddin, a family in Alexandria asked me to carry to their son just about to finish his Ph.D. in education at the University of Minnesota, he asked:

"What is this? Is it hashish?"

"No," I said. "It is a sheet of dried apricots that are rolled for use as a drink during the Holy month of Ramadan. The sheets are to be soaked in water during the day. After purification, you may add dried grapes, figs, and pine nuts. With a little sugar and rose water, you leave it chilled until sunset when Muslims break their fast. Would you like to try a piece?"

He was hesitant. "You take a piece and put it in your mouth first," he said.

I did so. After I showed him that it was harmless, he tore a part from the sheets himself. He reluctantly put it in his mouth and hesitantly chewed on it. He liked it and allowed the package to get in with me.

The ease by which we went through the customs and immigration was indeed astonishing to my fellow Egyptian travelers and me, coming from a country known for its long tedious and time consuming bureaucratic procedures.

After a pleasant interlude with other Egyptians in New York City, I took a TWA flight to Washington, D.C. As I was landing at National Airport, I saw the Washington Monument, the National Cathedral, the tower of Georgetown University, and the Potomac River. I headed directly to the YMCA at 18th & G Streets Northwest where I stayed for a couple of nights in an small, overheated room, no more than twelve by ten feet.

Before I came to the United States, I applied to be under the supervision of Egypt's Educational Bureau, mainly to facilitate money transfers. It was a two-story building located at 2200 Kalorama Road Northwest. I went up the few wide steps to its entrance that had the sign on the right hand side of the door: United Arab Republic Educational and Cultural Bureau. With the 1958 unification of Egypt and Syria culminating the ideology of Pan-Arabism that Nasser had strongly adopted and became a strong advocate of, he changed the official name of Egypt to United Arab Republic. When the unification of the two countries ended in 1961, the official name of Egypt changed to Arab Republic of Egypt. At the Bureau, Dr. Marawan greeted me warmly. He gave me a check in the amount of $200, and went out of his way to take me to a nearby bank to cash the money for me. I was delighted to note that the notorious time-consuming bureaucracy practiced in Egypt was not adopted by its officials abroad.

Friday March 11, 1960, was my last day in Washington, D.C. With Dr. Ali El-Refai, whom I met accidentally, we visited the White House at 1600 Pennsylvania Avenue. We were both surprised as to how small it was in comparison to the palaces of Abdeen, Kobba, Montaza, Rasettin and others belonging to our kings in Egypt before the 1952 revolution. From the White House, we walked to the Capitol Building. As we entered the neo-classical historical building, we thought that the building's guards were ushers standing to guide visitors whenever they needed information and to answer questions that people may pose. One of the uniformed personnel pointed out to me two famous senators walking by and engaging in a conversation with one another. One was Senator Everett McKinley Dirksen from Illinois with his deep vibrating voice and the other towering figure was Senator J. William Fulbright from Arkansas with his distinguished features. I was tempted to shake hands with them, but after quick hesitation, I decided not to interrupt. Years later, I had the distinctive pleasure of getting to know Senator Fulbright well. I worked with him especially after he left the Senate in 1974 until his death in 1995.

We then visited the Library of Congress. I walked into the beautifully decorated Library of Congress with its colorful tiles and stacks of millions of books, photographs, publications, manuscripts, maps and all other writing forms. I bowed to man's knowledge represented in just an insignificant portion at the world's largest library. It is always that feeling of true humility that comes upon me when I am surrounded by stacks of publications. It is a characteristic I am proud to have even if I am not in the presence of the majesty of knowledge. I wandered about downtown, seeing gigantic department stores such as Woodward & Lothrop and Garfinkel's. I asked a gentleman to guide me to the address I had for the Islamic Center on Massachusetts Avenue for the Friday prayer in its mosque. "Where is your car?" he asked. He took it for granted that I had an automobile. Sure enough, I learned that almost everyone had a car in the United States. Anis Mansour, a prominent writer in Egypt, commented on his visit to the United States that a car is like a pair of shoes for an American. The abundance of cars in the United States was mind-boggling, particularly for someone coming from a country where at that time there was one car for every one thousand inhabitants. I ended up taking a taxi whose driver happened to be an Indian Muslim on his way to the mosque. He did not charge me for the ride.

The mosque, located east on Massachusetts Avenue along the area called the Embassy Row overlooking the Rock Creek Parkway, is small in comparison to the ones we have in Egypt. Yet it is elegant and beautifully designed as one of the landmarks of the city. It was less than three years old when I first visited it. At its opening ceremony, President Eisenhower had praised the Islamic world's "tradition of learning and rich culture" which has "for centuries contributed to the building of civilization." As he said at the opening, "As I stand beneath these graceful arches, surrounded on every side by friends from far and near, I am convinced that our common goals are both right and promising. Faithful to the demands of justice and of brotherhood, each working according to the lights of his own conscience, our world must advance along the paths of peace."

The five arches at the mosque's entrance and five windows on each side reflect the five-time prayers as one of the five pillars of Islam.

Before the Friday prayer and after a recitation from the Holy Q'uran, the Imam at that time, Dr. Hobballah, a graduate form Al-

Azhar University in Cairo, gave his two sermons using the two languages, Arabic and English, since members of the Muslim community and visitors attending the prayer did not all know the Arabic language. In attendance there were nationals from Africa, the Arab world, Bangladesh, China, Europe, India, Indonesia, Iran, Pakistan, the Soviet Union, Turkey, the United States, and many others from the furthest corners of the world who happened to be in Washington.

In his sermon, Dr. Hobballah stressed the simplicity of Islam, the relationship between the person and God the creator without anyone in between. There is no celibacy in Islam as it stresses *jihad* for hard work for the betterment of oneself and those who one happens to take responsibility for. As in the other monotheistic religions, he urged Muslims to do whatever is good for themselves, their families, communities, nations and the world at large; but to avoid the bad, the forbidden, the unlawful and the harmful so that an afterlife reward would be given to good deeds while punishment could be applied to those who went astray: "Each one of you whether a ruler, a head of family or an employer is a shepherd and each of you is responsible for his/her own flock. Authority has to be exercised with responsibility in applying fairness and justice." Islam is a religion of peace, as the very word of Islam is a derivation of peace. "Salam alaykum," meaning "peace on you," is the common greeting when one Muslim meets another.

I enjoyed Washington. But I knew my encounter with the Americans had just begun.

I flew on a Northwest Airlines airplane with its well-known red tail from Washington at 9:00 a.m. on Saturday, March 12, 1960. I had a touch of cold and decided to move to the last row that had no passengers. Jennifer, an airline hostess, came by to see if I needed to hang my jacket, but while I was taking it off, a button fell off. She was so gracious as to pulling out a small sewing kit from her purse, and she stood by the corner of my seating row to fix it for me. She told me she was fascinated to have finally met an Egyptian, as one of her dreams was to visit Egypt. She kept talking with me while fixing the button. I had to blow my nose. So instead of reaching to my jacket to pull a handkerchief, I excused myself to go to the toilet.

Inside, I found different compartments. One was labeled "sanitary napkin." While my English was good, there were certain words I was not familiar with. I translated the unfamiliar phrase literally as "healthy clean napkin." I took a few, went to my seat, started to open one and got it close to my nose. All of that happened while she was still fixing the button looking with astonishment and bewilderment to what I was doing. I looked at it and realized what it was! Her eyes were getting wider and wider. I was embarrassed but smiled. Some time later, when she had a layover in Minneapolis, we went to dinner and later on I arranged through an Egyptian tourist office to fulfill her dream of visiting the country and its ancient monuments. While in Alexandria, my family hosted her for a couple of days.

As soon as I arrived at the Minneapolis International Airport, I headed towards a telephone booth to call Mohamed Selim, the brother of an old classmate of mine. As I was struggling to make the telephone call, Dr. and Mrs. Charles Porter came toward me and introduced themselves. He was a physics professor at the University of Minnesota, and he offered to give me a ride to the university. I passed the phone on to him so that he could negotiate where to drop me off. As soon as we walked out of the airport, walking slowly on the snow that covered everything, including tree branches, the lowest temperature I had ever experienced hit me.

The Porters gave me a lift to Dinkytown, within walking distance from the main campus. They dropped me at Bridgeman's, a corner store, where I waited for the gentleman I called from the airport. I had to check the expensive ring I had securely kept in my small trousers pocket. It was a gift from the Selim family in Egypt to his new wife. He soon arrived. I saw a gentleman almost six foot tall with a woolen hat, a warm coat and heavy gloves with fur lining. He came directly to me, because he recognized my distinctive black moustache.

"I am Mohamed Selim. You can call me Mo," he said. "Welcome to the below-freezing Minnesota weather."

"I am delighted to meet you," I replied. "I heard a lot about you from your younger brother, Hassan, who was my classmate at Ramleh Secondary School. I have been at your lovely corner villa and its spacious beautiful gardens facing the tramway tracks. Your brother Fawzy asked me to give you your family's wedding gift to your wife."

"Her name is Evelyn from Minnesota. She belongs to the arts world. You will see some of her paintings," he said. "If you do not have plans this evening, I wish to extend an invitation to you to join us for the birthday party of Cully Swanson, a good friend of ours. His wife Gertrude had arranged everything at their home but kept it as a surprise to her husband. I told her about you and she will welcome you if you can come."

Mo and I were bonded by an instantaneous friendship that grew over the years. We have kept in touch with one another for the past fifty years. Mo became a professor of economics at the College of Saint Thomas, where he stayed until he retired in 2005. After a cup of coffee, we walked in the bitterly cold weather to an apartment nearby. We knocked on the door, which was not locked—a telling sign of the openness of America. "Let me introduce you to Massis Yeterian, a microbiologist at the University of Minnesota St. Paul Campus. He is currently the President of the Arab-American Club," Mo said.

Massis was sitting on a large, soft armchair with a newspaper scattered all around him. The size of the *Minneapolis Star* was mind-boggling. Massis, originally an Armenian from Iraq, came to the United States when he was about thirteen. He spoke English with a perfect Midwestern American accent. His sense of humor, his distinctive laughter, his warmth, his early baldness and his quick mind are characteristics I observed throughout our lifelong friendship. Mo and Massis discussed the last preparations for an important speaker, Dr. Fayez Sayegh, who was to address the Arab-American Club soon at the University Coffman Memorial Union.

Mo drove me with my suitcases to Centennial Hall, where I stayed for a few months. From behind the counter, a clerk asked, "How can I help you?" The sentence is common in America, but was completely alien to my ears. In Egypt, clerks complicate matters unnecessarily and make it routine to procrastinate. I have been impressed ever since by the immediate rapport, friendliness, practicality, efficiency and simplicity of the Americans.

I walked in my room at 7109 Centennial Hall. It was an elongated one, 14 feet in length, 10 in width and 8 in height, with a small bed, a large closet, a desk, and some bookshelves. The room overlooked a side yard with snow covering the grounds and the trees. I did not discover how beautiful the different shades of greenery and well-designed landscaping were until snow melted by the end of May.

John McLoone IV, who lived two doors down the hall from me, came to introduce himself. He made an immediate impression. "I am an Irish American, and proud of the heritage of my ancestors," he announced. "I can assure you that one of us, John Kennedy, will be the President of United States come November."

He pulled out a chair and told me that he was heading for a party where there would be kegs of beer and many Irish friends. Having anticipated he would invite me to the party, I hastened to tell him that I had other plans that evening.

"We will have several encounters, as I am eager to know about the great history of your country. But for the time being, can I be of any help to you?" John said.

"I need to buy a warm hat with flaps to cover both ears and my neck in the back," I replied. "I was freezing when I walked a short distance, across the street in Dinkytown and from Mo's car to the entrance of Centennial Hall."

John was indeed helpful, and we set out to buy what I needed. As we talked along the way, I found out that he was writing his Ph.D. dissertation in philosophy on "James Joyce: A Philosopher?" Joyce's great literary contributions are familiar to all, but John meant to focus on Joyce as a philosopher. In the course of our conversation, he continued to bombard me with his pronouncements, like this one: "I want to teach you something about this country. People in the United States are divided in only two groups: Irish and those who would like to be." My first impression of John was that he was an arrogant, highly opinionated person. But I soon discovered that he had a heart of gold. We became good friends. Later on, his younger sister Mary became my student at Georgetown University in 1967.

As I was leaving him that afternoon before Mo would come to take me to a surprise birthday party, I said, "Thank you, John, for going out of your way to get me what I needed."

"Mmm-hmmm," he replied. I understood immediately that it was Midwestern for "you're welcome."

Because Mo had lived in the United States since 1953 and was married to an American from the Midwest, he was fully Americanized in his accent, appearance, actions and punctuality. As he told me before leaving, "I'll pick you up at 6:00 p.m." Watching from a window at a reception area and keeping my eye on a big clock high on the wall, I saw Mo pulling his car in front of the dormitory at six sharp. Mo was surprised to see how fast I had adapted to Minneapolis weather.

He admired my new, warm hat, and when he thanked me for bringing the ring, I found myself replying "Mmm-hmmm."

He laughed and said, "You are a quick learner. Welcome to the world of the Midwest."

When we arrived at the home where the party was held, we were quietly ushered to a back room until a signal was to be given to us. We all shouted, "Surprise!" as we entered into a dining room where Cully was quietly sitting. We sang happy birthday to his 77th birthday when his wife Gertrude carried a big cake with 77 candles to blow.

Cully Swanson owned a funeral home and was at that time serving his term as the Potentate of a charitable organization for fellowship and good cause called the Shriners. Mo, Massis, our friend Shukri Ibrahim, and I were admiring Cully's standing in the community and the service he rendered to children. But at the same time we were surprised and amused by his profession as the person who buries the dead. What a world of difference between a *hanouti* in Egypt, who had no standing in the community, and the Swansons, the owners of an elaborate burial home. Gertrude Swanson was a formidable dynamic lady with a superb organizational talent. She was tall and slender with quick movements and a sharp mind. She had an interest in foreign students and opened her doors—and her refrigerator—to them at all times. She was elected the Vice President of People to People Organization with President Dwight D. Eisenhower as the Honorary Chairman. As my relationship with the Swansons grew over the years until their death, she appointed me to the Board of Trustees of People to People Organization, an international organization dedicated to reaching out to people wherever they are around the globe.

My first evening in Minneapolis was a springboard from which

I dove into the sea of an American way of life from the onset. It was rich and enjoyable. That was the America to which I was introduced, the America that used to be loved everywhere.

I soon began my studies. Edward Coen, an international economist, was assigned to me as my academic advisor. On the way to see him, I ran into Leonid Hurwicz, a famous econometrician, statistician and theorist. At my meeting with him, I felt that I was in the presence of a genius. He told me the specialization of each faculty. While we were talking, Walter Heller dropped by. He was a tall, distinguished gentleman who reminded me of a British lord.

"Walter, this is Ib Oweiss, who almost finished his master's degree at Alexandria University in Egypt, but came here to obtain a Ph.D. His area of interest is international trade," Hurwicz introduced me.

"Welcome to the University of Minnesota," Heller said. "Can you drop by to see me after your meeting with your faculty advisor?"

When I met Heller in his office, he showered me with lots of questions concerning Egyptian antiquities since he was thinking of traveling to Egypt some time in December 1961. His plans changed after he was chosen by President John F. Kennedy to head his Council of Economic Advisors soon thereafter.

The next day, I ran into Professor Hurwicz again. He looked at me and asked, "Whatever happened to the thick black moustache you had yesterday?"

"When in Rome do like the Romans do," I replied. "Since I came to the United States, I did not see any man with a moustache so I decided to be like the rest of you and shaved it off this morning."

"I predict that you will do very well in this country. You adapt very quickly," he said.

I was later Hurwicz's student in upper graduate courses and an avid reader of his work. I thought to myself that he would one day become a Nobel Laureate. In fact, my prediction came true as he was awarded in 2007 the Nobel Prize in economics, one year before he died at age 90.

* * *

Between my studies and my involvement in speeches and debates in addition to my limited social life, I had to find a part-time job, since the salary I got from the Ministry of Industry through the Egyptian Educational Bureau in Washington, D.C., would last only for a few months. The leave of absence with pay granted by the Ministry of Industry was only for nine months. Since the available position I found was to wash dishes at Centennial Hall to pay for my room and board, I chose the early hours from 5:30 to 7:00 a.m. so that I would not be seen. In my status back home, it would be shameful and unacceptable to wash dishes. Now, I recall it with pride.

I sailed through my studies easily as I was well prepared in the field of economics in both my undergraduate and postgraduate studies in Egypt. I received straight A's in all the courses I took and outstanding comments on my term papers. Just one year after my arrival in the United States, I earned my masters degree. Professor Bronfenbrenner, who left the most profound impact on me, summoned me to his office.

"Congratulations on your outstanding performance," he said. "I nominated you to the faculty of the Department of Economics to teach micro- and macroeconomics. It was voted unanimously in your favor. Would you accept?"

"Do you think that my English is good enough to teach Americans?" I asked.

"You know my language. I do not know yours. Besides, your English is superior in comparison to that of many native speakers," he replied.

With a sigh of relief and a sense of accomplishment, I agreed. The amount of money I earned was sufficient to pay for my books, for my room and board, and for all other needed expenses without having to wash dishes anymore.

At the beginning of each class, I give the title of the course, my name and my office hours. I also say proudly that I was born and raised in Egypt. It was at the beginning of my teaching career in the United States, one of my students came to see me after class.

"My name is Ted Sherr. I am Jewish. I wish to withdraw from your class because you are Egyptian. You may treat me differently from the rest of the class," he said.

I replied carefully: "My neighbor in Alexandria is Jewish. We lived together amicably and friendly in all of my growing years. I am against Zionism as are other Jews," I said. "But I am not anti-Semitic, simply because I am myself a Semite. I urge you to continue in my class and will be delighted to help you academically as I do all others without differentiation."

As it turned out, Ted stayed in my class and earned an A. As years passed by, he became a dear friend. To my pleasure, upon finishing his graduate studies, he was offered a job as a statistician with the U.S. Energy Commission not far away from Washington, D.C., after I accepted an offer to teach at Georgetown University. He found an apartment not far from where I used to live in Arlington. On weekends, we sampled food at different restaurants. I introduced him to Marialyce, my neighbor at the Arlington Towers. She is a Catholic from Boston, with a typical Bostonian accent. They fell in love with one another and got married. We kept in touch over the years even after they moved to Europe when he was appointed to the U.S. team with the United Nations International Atomic Energy Agency headquartered in Vienna. It was established in 1946 with the original purpose of peaceful atomic energy and the elimination of weapons of mass destruction. The Agency and its Egyptian Director-General, Mohamed ElBaradei, shared the 2005 Nobel Prize for Peace.

I soon felt that Minneapolis was my home. The warmth of the people of Minnesota had more than compensated for its frigid winters. I came to love the Americans through the Billmans, the Swansons, the Moors, the Dahlners, the Petersons, the Andersons and the many others I met in Minnesota.

Their warmth touched me in many ways. Upon learning in 1966 that my 3-year-old nephew, Hamada, contracted polio in Alexandria, Egypt, I was overwhelmed by the people's generosity. Gertrude Swanson through her People to People organization and her husband's Cully as the Minneapolis Shrines' Potentate raised the necessary funds to bring him over together with his aunt, my sister Fatma, to the University of Minnesota Hospital after having secured his treatment through a research grant since there was no spotted case of polio in the United States to study. Hamada was a delightful boy with an attractive smile. He was a heart breaker. Everyone loved him even though he did not know English when he first arrived. The arrangement was that he would stay at the hospital throughout the week, but he would spend the weekends with my sister and me in my flat just across the street from the hospital in Delaware Street. His nurses asked me to write a mini dictionary for Arabic words such as "water," "eat," "sleep," "rest," "extend your legs," and others to be written phonetically in the English alphabet. He was given toys and was introduced to American television. In less than six weeks, his nurses informed me that they did not need the dictionary since he had quickly learned to speak English with an American accent.

One weekend, I had several Arabs congregating in my small apartment including a famous cinema star, Lubna Abdel-Aziz, who was married to Egyptian physician Ismail Barrada doing some training at a medical hospital in Saint Paul. My colleague from the economics department, Alice Hall from Richmond, Virginia, with her notable southern accent, fell in love with Hamada. He sat on her lap and kept translating to her what all others were saying in Arabic. It was an amazing experience for a quick learner at that young age. He stayed for about six months and was given special crutches. He was taught how to depend on himself given that his leg muscles were destroyed when he was attacked by the poliovirus. Hence, there was nothing left to build upon. Shortly after we celebrated his fourth birthday, many of his Minnesota friends accompanied him and my sister to Minneapolis airport in a cold winter day in February 1967. A friend who was driving a taxi to pay for his tuition had his working hat on. Hamada said, "Hi, cab driver!" He was a joy.

In addition to the Americans, I had many other close friends with whom I still keep in touch. One time, I volunteered to baby-sit for Mo and Evelyn's children so that they could go to a movie. It was about Christmas time with several decorations around a fireplace done artistically, and a large Christmas tree in a corner with flashing lights and wrapped gifts in different attractive colors tossed underneath. Their son Ali, who was five years old at the time, told me, "I want to tell you something. I know that Santa does not exist and can never come down through our chimney while we would be sleeping. There is no sleigh ride carrying him from the North Pole as we were told. But please do not tell my parents, I enjoy receiving their gifts."

As it turned out later on, that bright, witty Ali in partnership with his wife Robin became well-known TV producers and film-makers. His film *Sweet Land* is a love story of two Scandinavian immigrant farmers to southern Minnesota after World War I. The film critic Leonard Maltin put it in his book of *The 151 Best Movies You've Never Seen*.

It was in Minnesota, where I spent the first seven years in the United States, that I was introduced to peanut butter sandwiches and learned how to wash it down with milk when it gets stuck in the upper part of the mouth. I have been eating it occasionally, especially the crunchy one, ever since. I also learned how to ski.

Another winter sport I learned in the freezing Minnesota weather was ice sailing. Russ Johnson, a native of Minnesota of Swedish descent, who married a Norwegian in spite of a cultural rivalry between their ancestors, invited me to ice-skate on a frozen lake. The Johnsons came in their Cadillac with a trailer hooked to the car. The trailer carried a 25-foot sailboat with all its masts down. With its one long blade centered at its bottom, the boat was securely fastened on eight rubber wheels on each of its two sides. When we arrived at Lake Minnetonka, the very same lake in which I swam in the summer, Russ drove on the lake to my amazement and surprise. Russ assured me as a renowned engineer that it is utterly safe to drive on top of the frozen lake. It did not take long to crank down the boat from the trailer and prepare it for sailing. With the masts up, Russ and his wife skillfully sailed, even as the temperature reached -40 degrees Fahrenheit. It was a unique experience for an Egyptian.

In the fall of 1961, I was elected the President of the Arab-American Club in the Twin Cities, with Khalid Ishaq, a pharmacologist from Iraq, as the Vice President and Mary Rush, a librarian from Minnesota, as the secretary. We had an ongoing program of lectures, tours and briefings.

I learned from Yahya Armajani, a historian at Macalester College, that Fayez Sayegh would be joining the faculty for the academic year 1962–63 to teach, to give four public lectures and to

pursue his academic research and publications. We were mesmer-
ized by his four lectures on the subject of neutralism, of which the
first was devoted fully to the definition of non-alignment between
the two superpowers at that time, the United States and the Soviet
Union.

I had carried with me a few copies of his study of the Arab-Israeli
conflict on my way to the United States, and so I was fortunate to
get to know him. We became close friends and remained so until his
death. He was a prolific writer, a distinguished educator, teaching
at Oxford University and others places, and a prominent diplomat.
As a member of the Kuwaiti Delegation to the United Nations, he
was the author of the famous resolution equating Zionism with
racism until the United States used its power to nullify it. Because
of its brevity, clarity and objectivity, that study was my reference
for the last fifty years. I used it with our friends on the boat who
were eager to know about such a major conflict in the modern
history of the Middle East.

When I heard that Andrew I. Killgore, a career diplomat from
the Department of State, planned to visit Minneapolis I extended
an invitation to him to speak at the Arab-American Club. The following was what he wrote in *The Washington Report On Middle East
Affairs,* in the December 2005 issue:

> I met Dr. Sayegh in 1963 at the University of Minnesota,
> where I was giving a speech on the Middle East, particu-
> larly on the Arab-Israeli dispute. At that time the American
> media had been making much of Egyptian President Gamal
> Abdel Nasser's imaginary program to build rockets to fire
> at Israel. Egypt was being assisted by German scientists, ac-
> cording to the American press.
>
> The moment I finished my remarks, a young man leapt
> to his feet to ask furiously, "Mr. Killgore, when will the
> United States make Nasser get rid of his Nazi scientists?"
>
> Immediately another man in the back of the room was
> on his feet to say, "Mr. Killgore, let me answer that ques-
> tion. Nasser will get rid of his Nazi scientists when the U.S.
> gets rid of its Nazi scientists." (The reference, of course, was
> to Werner von Braun and other German rocket scientists

whom Washington had brought to the U.S. from Germany at the end of World War II to help with our space program.)

Applause greeted the short and insightful observation, and no more was heard of so-called Nazi scientists. The man who so helpfully answered the surprise questioner was the distinguished professor Dr. Fayez Sayegh, who was teaching that year at Macalester College in nearby St. Paul. I accepted his invitation to speak to some of his classes at Macalester, delaying my return to Washington and the State Department by a day, and spent that delightful extra day in Minnesota with a brilliant man. I was struck not only by his intellectual prowess but also by his personal warmth, humor and humility. Although I never saw him again, I followed his career via press reports and through his writings.

As it turned out, Andy Killgore and I became good friends after I moved to Washington, D.C. and had invited him to serve on the board of The Council of Egyptian-American Relations that I established in 1999. He was a diplomat in several Arab capitals including Beirut, Jerusalem, Amman, Baghdad and Manama and was a desk officer in other Near East and South Asia regional bureau at the State Department in Washington before he was assigned as U.S. ambassador to Qatar. He is the publisher of *Washington Report On Middle East Affairs*, the most reliable and factual American magazine on the Middle East.

My time was devoted to teaching, scholarly work, involvement with the community, be it American, Arab or otherwise international, public speaking and an active role in informing Americans about Egypt, the Arab world and the misunderstood reality about the Arab-Israeli conflict.

An event that has been rooted in my memory reflected the generosity of the American people. When I was president of the Arab-American Club I made a plea in Owatonna, Minnesota, for desperately needed blankets for the Algerian-war refugees. Under the chairmanship of Mrs. Clarence Kaplan, a committee for the blanket drive was formed including Reverend Jack Berry, rector of St. Paul's Episcopal Church, Mayor of Owatonna Kenneth Austin, Mrs. Austin and me. Mrs. Kaplan organized a well attended event

at the ballroom of the Hotel Owatonna in which I thanked the donors. It was stated in an article appearing in the *Owatonna Peoples
Press*:

> Oweiss expressed astonishment that an American city so far
> away should be concerned about the suffering of Algerians.
> He told fellow dinner guests of the appalling situation of
> the thousands of Algerian refugees fleeing from air raids on
> their villages. Those people found their homes ransacked
> and burnt upon their return. They became homeless and
> destitute refugees through no fault of their own. Because of
> the great need for blankets and warm clothes the drive has
> been extended through December 22, 1962. Contributions
> may be left at the Baptist church, west door, by Saturday.

At the function held in honor of Fayez Sayegh as the distinguished speaker shortly after I arrived in Minneapolis, I met Noël
Vreeland, a 19-year-old enthusiastic woman who came from New
York to study Egyptology at the University of Minnesota. We often bumped into one another either in Dinkytown or on the main
campus. Over a warm cup of coffee at Bridgeman's, she asked me
questions about Egypt, the ancient history of the Pharaohs, Alexandria where I grew up and, of course, myself. In talking about
Alexandria, I translated to her a poem I wrote describing its charm.
She was fascinated and encouraged me to write poetry in English
as well. I did. In spite of the eight years separating us in age, we became close to one another. I used to walk her to her room in the International House. She accompanied me to several functions, joining my activism for fairness and understanding of the complexities
of the Middle East problems.

The more I got to know her, the closer we became to one another. We read poetry to one another or discussed a wide range
of topics of mutual interest. We went to picnics on summer days
by Lake Como spreading blankets on the beach by the waterfront,
enjoying the food and drinks we carried along with us. We canoed
on the quiet reflective water with weeping willows that grew on a
little island in the middle of the lake. Some branches were barely
kissing the surface of the water, while others were submerged or

were dancing with tickles of gentle breeze, while their shadows on the quiet surface of the lake kept trailing us wherever we canoed around.

Noël was short and had gleaming eyes, rosy, rounded cheeks and smiles that made the whole world around us seem to brighten. She was beautiful inside and out. She spoke her mind and from the heart. She had only one sister, fourteen years older than she. The poor girl had to suffer riding with me in my dusty beaten up 1949 Ford with its partially rusted floor allowing winter cold air to pierce to our bones. One time, I could not recognize the car I kept looking for in a huge open parking lot, until I saw a Ford of the same color but clean. It was my car. Noël decided in my absence to clean it on a hot summer day. When she wrote her first book, *The Lazarus Curse*, the car was on her mind. She wrote of the "dusty black hood of the Ford" while commenting herself in a note accompanying the book, "the poor old car was always dusty." We laughed about it, cracking many jokes with our close friends. We were happy together sharing volunteer work for the community, going to concerts at Northrop Auditorium, enjoying movies, attending public lectures at Coffman Union, or simply being together. We had an unforgettable romance.

After a year and a half, Noël had to go back East. I was heartbroken. She met in New York a known writer in the world of science fiction. She got married and became Noël Vreeland Carter. She never once forgot to send me a cheerful note on the occasion of my birthday. In her book, *Miss Hungerford's Handsome Hero*, Noël kept a scene in the back of her memory when she sewed the loose button on the camel hair coat that my generous brother Mohamed had given me.

In the spring of 1967, I was offered a high position in Egypt. I was nostalgic of the old country and felt home sick for my family. I resigned my position at the University of Minnesota and gave my landlord, Mr. Gould, a notice that I planned to vacate my apartment by the end of the summer. I finished the spring semester but signed up to teach summer school to enable me to purchase the gifts I would need to take along with me.

During the summer session, the 1967 Arab-Israeli War broke out. We sat glued to television while trying to listen to Cairo Radio where there was a station called Sawt El-Arab, meaning "The Arab Voice." Its announcer was Ahmed Said with his deep loud voice full of emotional rhetoric. We heard Ahmed Said saying, "We shot down 200 Israeli planes," and after a while, he would increase the number, while we saw the real story on the American networks ABC, CBS and NBC. Ahmed Said gave his big fat lies at a time when world news coming also from BBC and others gave an exact opposite picture. The Israelis planned the surprise attack on the Egyptian Air Force and wiped them out on the ground before Field Marshall Abdel-Hakim Amer, the confidante of President Nasser in charge of Egyptian forces, woke up. With no air defense, the Israeli ground forces moved quickly and occupied the entire Sinai Peninsula all the way to the Suez Canal where some of their soldiers jumped to swim in its waters carrying their rifles, a sign for victory. It was a lightning victory for the Israelis but a shameful defeat for Nasser and his regime.

That war had a devastating effect on many of us thousands of miles away from our home countries. In my speeches and media interviews, I condemned Israel for its aggression and occupying other Arab lands rather than seeking peaceful co-existence. It created more complexities in the Arab-Israeli disputes than the already existing ones. In the meanwhile, I voiced my opinion concerning the failure of Nasser and his regime. I found his slogans to be hollow and without substance. He kept saying, "We manufactured from the needle to the missile." As it turned out, neither one was effectively produced.

Having attacked Nasser openly, it was not possible for me to return to Egypt, and so I began looking for an academic post in the United States. I was invited to give seminars to the faculty of economics both in the east and west coasts for the possibility of teaching at their institutions. All of my trips were interesting, but my interview in Cincinnati stands out. A professor from the department of economics volunteered to pick me up from the airport. After I finished giving my seminar, the chairman insisted he would drive me back to the airport himself. On the way, he informed me he summoned the whole department for a short meeting after my seminar. It was unanimously voted that the chairman should make me an attractive offer to teach in the fall.

He was a nice gentleman and a good economist but a lousy driver. He kept moving his head towards me when he wanted to get my attention. I became nervous while he was driving on a narrow two-way road. There was a slow moving car ahead of us. He speeded to pass it, but saw an incoming taxi that opted not to give him a chance. Instead of slowing down to get back behind the slow-moving vehicle, he pressed his foot on the accelerator and moved quickly back on the right lane before the incoming taxi would hit us. He lost control as he was heading beyond the paved road to an agricultural land, turned his wheel to the left, passed the incoming lane and drove diagonally on the grass for about two hundred feet. We barely missed a tree and instead hit a house, landing partially inside a garage. We were both fine, but we heard a moaning from inside the house. It was an old lady who, having noticed from her bedside window that a car was coming in the direction of her house, tried to get off her bed but fell on the floor. Luckily, we were told she was not hurt. When I got out of the car with some blood on my face, the chairman pulled himself out as well. Some people in the area gathered around us quickly. One of them told me, "You should be dead." Fortunately, not all of my seminars were so memorable.

I got offers to teach at the University of Cincinnati, Georgetown University, the University of San Francisco, and Yale University. I was torn to choose between the latter three. Yale had great minds, but I found the city of New Haven depressing. The two places that attracted me the most were San Francisco and Washington, D.C.

I stayed longer in the latter to inhale more of its air and to know more about the university than I could get in a short visit. I walked through the streets of the attractive Georgetown neighborhood evaluating my overall impressions of the place. Was it an environment in which I could spend years, or even decades? It was in front of the impressive Healy Building, as I walked through the decorative iron-wrought gates of Georgetown University at the intersection of 35th and O Streets and passed the statue of Father Healy sitting in a chair giving an aura of learning and peace, that I made my decision. I would accept the offer. I would be a professor at Georgetown University.

* * *

On a sunny summer day in 1967, I packed up my car with all of my personal belongings for the trip to the East Coast. I had already shipped my furniture ahead of me so that it would be there when I arrived in Washington.

Before my departure, I put a note on the bulletin board of Coffman Memorial Union offering a free ride to Washington in exchange for helping out in driving part of the road. One young woman took me up on the offer. She was headed to a job interview in Maryland after having finished her master's degree in psychology. We thought of making the trip to Washington in a couple of days by driving as many miles we could each day. Driving a long distance on highways in the United States soon becomes monotonous. To pass time, I brought a stack of tapes of Arab composers and singers. But my companion did not know Arabic, and so we listened to Beethoven and Mozart instead. She was knowledgeable about the two great composers. She was wondering why some become geniuses while the majority of people hover at average or above average, not to mention the below average or retarded. In her field of psychology, she studied statistics, so when I explained to her the concept of normal curves, she quite understood the range of abilities to the right and left of any particular center.

As we pulled out from the highway, the many flickering lights of motels, gas stations, shops and advertisements of different sizes and shapes turned night into day. My companion was tall with thin lips and hard features. She must have noticed that I was not attracted to her. Yet she had other plans in mind. On the way, she asked if she could share a room with me to save money. We chose what seemed from the outside as a good motel. I left her in the car while walking to the entrance of a well-lit office. I paid for a room with two beds for one night, went back to the car and drove until I parked in front of our room. I advised her to take only a few items needed for the night, but instead she decided to take her heavy suitcase in the room. I had to carry it for her. She asked me to put it flat on one of the beds.

I left her for about twenty minutes during which time I stretched my legs and bought a soda from a vending machine. When I came back, I found that she had emptied most of her clothes except books on one bed while she was still taking a bath. Even though I wanted to go to sleep, I stepped out of the room again for few minutes to give her privacy. I picked up the town newspaper and glanced over its headlines. As I expected, it reflected the provincial nature of the town. There was no mention of international events. As I entered our room, I was overtaken by the odor of a pleasant perfume. Only one, dim light was on. My companion had covered herself with a thin white sheet and asked me with a sweet voice to join her and started to show her affection towards me telling me how much she admired my personality, character and sense of humor. After a while, I could not resist her exciting temptation, and we slept in each other's arms.

I woke up early, did my pushups, took a shower, and got dressed. I walked out to the motel's office to get coffee with cakes and fruit for both of us and went back to our room to wake her up and to serve her breakfast in bed. It was a late start by the time she repacked and got ready for the trip. My companion noticed that I was displeased at her lack of consideration for my desire to start early and asked me if she can take her turn driving the first leg of the trip. We talked about a mutual friend for a while, but she continually changed the subject to ask about me. Every time I answered, she would pose a question, "Why do you say that?" I grew irritated, but her questions accelerated. At first, I gave long answers to consume some time, but as her questions accelerated, I gave briefer and sharper answers. A thought crossed my mind of the female scorpion that poisons its male after mating. After a while, it became unbearable to listen to her. If I turned on the radio, or tried to put a tape on, she would turn it off. "Don't you want to listen to me?" she asked. I could not believe that she was the same person who showed me her affections the night before.

I thought of Jean-Paul Sartre's play, *No Exit*, and his view that hell is other people. I was trapped with this woman in one car for two days. I turned off my ears and meditated instead of listening to her, thinking of memories of Minnesota at times, and Alexandria with my family, childhood and experiences at others. As soon as I dropped her off at the address she wanted to go to, I let out a huge sigh of relief. I never saw her again.

2

Family and Faith

On the first Saturday in May 1974, I decided to go to a nearby Safeway store in north Arlington to buy a couple of snacks. At the cashier's, there was a young lady in her early thirties ahead of me with a basket full of groceries. With an elegant hat on her head, she turned to me noticing that I had a few items in my hands and said in a noticeable French accent, "Please go ahead of me." I nodded at her kind gesture and proceeded. She has been in trouble ever since for one simple reason. Reader, I married her.

She stood five foot five inches tall with red cheeks, a beautiful face, and green eyes. She showed exquisite taste in the dress and the hat she was wearing. One week later, I met her coincidentally at the same Safeway store examining the contents of the same can we were each about to buy. We nodded to each other and left.

A few days later as I was walking from my office at Georgetown University on the second floor of the Nevils building on my way to a meeting with the chairman of the department of economics, I ran again into what I thought to be a French lady for the third time. I asked her, "What are you doing here?" She replied with a sweet smile, "I am a graduate student in French literature."

"But this is unfair to other students," I objected. "Being French, you have a comparative advantage over others in your class."

"Pardon me," she replied. "I am not French. I am Belgian from the French speaking part."

After introducing myself while extending my hand to her, she said, "I am Mrs. Lamb." Having observed some sort of disappointment in my look and realizing that it may have been the end of it as far as I was concerned, she quickly added, "But I am divorced. My name is Céline Marie-Joseph Lesuisse." I then invited her for a drink at the Tombs across the street from our office building. She told me she had been married but never had children. Her former husband was originally from Pennsylvania but was stationed in Belgium where they met and got married. He returned to the United States bringing along his bride to pursue his studies at George Washington Law School. Shortly after she arrived in Washington in 1972, Céline started teaching mathematics and then French language at Gonzaga High School, but decided to pursue a graduate degree in French literature after she was divorced. Ten years earlier, she had earned a masters degree in Belgium upon completion of her thesis on quantum mechanics.

The more I talked to her, the more I found in her the attractive features of a woman I could marry. Just prior to meeting her, I had resigned myself to the fact that I might have to live as a bachelor for the rest of my life. As man gets older, his demands increase while the choices open to him become less and less as the suitable ones already got married. My young brother Zakaria, whom I had brought from Egypt, lived with me and kept encouraging me to marry her.

Upon learning that my 72-year-old father, then diabetic for ten years, had had one of his legs amputated because of injury complications in his foot, I flew to Egypt. From the only international airport in Cairo at the time, I took a limousine directly to Alexandria some 150 miles away. My father was lying in bed in our villa in Victoria while my mother was sitting on the opposite bed. After warm greetings, hugs and tears, he looked at me ad said, "My son, you have thus far accomplished a lot in the United States, but an important part of your life is missing. When are you getting married?"

In the few months after I met Céline a budding flower of love started to grow in both of our hearts. "My dear father, I met a superb person that I wish to marry. She is Catholic and originally from Belgium," I said, and showed them her picture.

"Prophet Muhammad married Maria, an Egyptian Christian Copt. You have our blessings. May God bestow happiness upon both of you!" my father said. He added, "My advice to you is never to attempt to convert her to Islam unless she herself becomes convinced and wants voluntarily to become a Muslim."

It took me a while to decide on such a major step in my life. Having made up my mind, I rushed to the home of a very close friend, Ambassador Ashraf Ghorbal, with one of Céline's rings concealed in my pocket. I thought of asking his wife Amal to come with me to buy an engagement ring. She was not at home but their daughter Nahed, who was a student of mine at Georgetown University, was, and she accompanied me to a jewelry store to help me find a ring.

I invited her to dinner at my apartment on her 35th birthday, on April 20, 1975. I chose some soft music and a few French songs. From time to time, I invited her to dance throughout the duration of our meal. Following dessert and coffee, I brought out three gifts with the smallest on top to be opened last. The large one at the bottom was a crystal vase. The second was an Egyptian bracelet. When she opened the third box and saw a gold ring, she did not understand the meaning of the gift, as I had expected. She asked in French, "Qu'est-ce que c'est que ça?" — "What is this?" As I was explaining, I slipped it in the ring finger of her right hand. With overwhelming joy, she embraced me, while saying "Yes, yes" with tears running down her rosy cheeks when I proposed to marry her.

I moved quickly to prepare for the new phase of my life and kept looking for a house to buy. My close friends, Fernand Dahan, a prominent architect originally from Alexandria, Egypt, and his kind wife Anita, originally from Chile, invited me for a typical *sham-ennisim* breakfast. It was a national day enjoyed by all Egyptians regardless of their religious affiliation celebrating the beginning of the spring. Céline was also invited but she drove her own car after her early class at Gonzaga. On the way back she drove behind me in Kensington, Maryland, on Connecticut Avenue until I saw a sign being put up at the intersection of Glenridge Street. We saw the house with its five bedrooms on the second floor, and the reception and dining rooms as well as a spacious family room and large kitchen on the first floor. In addition, there was a full one-bedroom apartment with its own bathroom in the basement along with a utility room and a storage area. In the backyard, a medium size swimming pool was built in the midst of a beautifully designed landscaping and surrounded by trees giving a natural privacy to the residence. Céline looked at me and said in her distinguished French accent, "But it is too big!" Not only did I buy the house, I in fact doubled its size fifteen years later. I love space.

The official wedding took place at the Islamic Center on Massachusetts Avenue in its beautiful mosque. Dr. Mohamed Abdel-Rauf sat on a chair at the head of a small table while Céline and I sat facing each other on the right and left of the Imam. With a wide handkerchief covering the holding hands of both of us, he asked each one of us if we accepted marrying each other and declared us husband and wife. It was a simple ceremony and was duly witnessed and signed before the invited guests sitting on the superb Persian rugs donated originally by the Shah of Iran. Most of the Arab ambassadors (except Ashraf Ghorbal, Egypt's envoy, as he was in Egypt), our colleagues, and friends attended the exchange of vows. Around our swimming pool a reception was held for all of our guests. Dinner was graciously catered by two friends, Marilyn Murphy, the wife of my colleague Edward Murphy, and Patricia Dinkelacker, the wife of another colleague of mine, Bill Dinkelacker. My eldest brother Yousef, a lawyer at Egypt's Supreme Court, and his daughter Laila flew from Egypt to attend the wedding. My sister Fatma, her husband Ibrahim Elbarbary, and their 2-year-old daughter drove from Binghamton, New York, where they resided until he finished his Ph.D. in chemistry. My younger brother Zakaria, who lived with us until finishing his residency in obstetrics and gynecology at the Washington Hospital Center, filled the event with his lively humor and gracious hospitality.

We had only one-night's reservation at a nearby hotel. Our honeymoon was to be postponed to the following summer. My brother Zakaria recounted to us the following day that after we left my schoolmate Fouad Aly Hassan rushed inside the house to take off his clothes and with a long white towel around his bathing suit walked towards the swimming pool with his thin legs like Mahatma Gandhi and plunged in the pool. Someone else attempted to throw his female companion in the pool, and she laughingly said lifting her dress, "As you see, I am prepared—I have my bathing suit on." It was an enjoyable evening for everyone. Some even performed a traditional belly dance. When Ambassador Ghorbal returned to Washington, he insisted on hosting another full-fledged wedding party for us at the Egyptian Embassy at the Sheridan Circle, with its majestic entrance and beautifully decorated residency with walls of some historical pictures and colorful paintings, a good mix between the works of Egyptian artists and others.

Years later, when I was working for the Egyptian mission at the United Nations in New York, we wanted to start a family but encountered difficulties. We found out that the productive cycle of a woman of 37 who had not had children may be disturbed. Dr. Dessouky Ahmed Dessouky, her gynecologist and obstetrician, a professor of medicine at Georgetown University, advised her to see the top man in the field, Howard Jones, Jr., a professor at the Johns Hopkins University School of Medicine. Because of the long waiting time of several months, my able assistant, Cindy Pherson, called his secretary and told her, "Ambassador Oweiss wants to speak with Dr. Howard Jones." It took a few minutes, but she got him on the phone.

"It will be appreciated if you can give my wife an appointment at your earliest convenience," I said.

"What seems to be the problem?" he asked.

"We've wanted to start a family ever since we got married three years ago—"

"How old is she?"

"Thirty-seven."

"I wish she were ten years younger," he said. "Can you bring her to my office the day after tomorrow?"

We were elated. We found Dr. Jones to be a truly distinguished and accomplished man of 67. Together with his wife, Georgeanna Segar Jones, also a prominent gynecologist and obstetrician, they had invented a medication that would correct a woman's cycle. Céline went through several injections and pregnancy occurred. What a joyful moment it was when we found out! We were blessed by Yasmeen's birth on January 12, 1979. After a first baby is born a woman's cycle returns to normalcy. We had a boy named Kareem fifteen months later.

Instead of living by herself at her home in Brussels, Belgium, Céline's 70-year-old mother, Zelia Jacoby, decided to sell her property and come to live with us, which she did until her death in 1987. She was a totally devoted grandmother and took care of the children. The only language she spoke was French. With my busy schedule outside the home and travels abroad, the first language the children learned to speak was French. Of course, they picked up the English language even before they went school from *Sesame*

Street, Mr. Roger's Neighborhood, and *Captain Kangaroo.* Her life was her family, including her son Joseph and his wife Béatrice. She developed a real admiration and love for me when she lived with us. Before she died, she murmured, "Mission accomplie … les enfants … Ibrahim est gentil." ("Mission accomplished … the children … Ibrahim is gentle.")

My son's and daughter's childhood years are engraved in my memory. Within walking distance from our home in Kensington, I taught Yasmeen and Kareem how to fly a kite in the large parking lot of the school and church of Holy Redeemer, how to ride a bike in spite of many falls leaving bruises sometimes, taking them to soccer fields, preparing the grounds with marked boundaries before they start playing, being a linesman, cheering for their teams and encouraging them to score and rushing to carry them when they were hurt.

We capitalized on their having acquired a mother tongue in the French language. We enrolled Yasmeen and Kareem in the Lycée Rochambeau not far from our home. After having anchored a foreign language in their minds, we decided to transfer them to a private American school. We believed that as they were born in the United States, they should always be proud of their own heritage culturally and emotionally. They should be raised as good American citizens. In the meanwhile, we made them aware all long of the rich culture and deep roots of the countries of their parents through reading books, watching videos and direct exposure through several trips. I have always thought the best investment for the children is education no matter what the cost might be. Therefore, we decided to put them in the best possible private schools. Accordingly, Yasmeen went to Stone Ridge, an all-girls school, and afterwards enrolled at Georgetown University with a double major in English and psychology. Kareem went to Mater Dei, a private elementary school for boys, to St. Albans School at the Washington National Cathedral for high school, and later he, too, enrolled at Georgetown, majoring in culture and politics.

We thought that travel could complement their schooling and provide an additional source of information and understanding of other peoples and cultures. We took them to Egypt three times:

once when they were less than ten years old, once as teenagers, and once after they had graduated from college and been married. They also came with us twice to Europe visiting Belgium, France, and the United Kingdom.

In Belgium, we stayed with my brother-in-law Joseph Lesuisse and his wife Beatrice Mattheys, once when they were young at their apartment close to downtown Brussels and another at Everbeek, about forty miles north of Brussels, where one is awakened by cows mooing, roosters cock-a-doodle doo at dawn, followed by the sound of farmers' wagons pulled by horses or donkeys on their way to work at farms shortly after sunrise. In addition to our tour of Brussels, including the headquarters of the European Union, Joseph drove us north through the beautiful countryside of Holland with flowers shown on every balcony until we reached a pier where he docked his 30-foot sailboat. The North Sea was—as usual— dark and not very exciting.

We flew to Paris to visit its great landmarks, before they did so several more times as adults. We visited the Louvre where we spent hours enjoying its rare collection of paintings, sculptures and some ancient Egyptian acquisitions in a majestic and impressive display. Having read the *The Hunchback of Notre Dame* by Victor Hugo, it was memorable for our children to climb the height of Notre Dame Cathedral remembering the tragedy of the deformed Quasimodo. We had a breathtaking view of the Seine river and its surroundings. Paris is the city of charm and beauty, be it at the high plateau of Montmartre with its artists, coffee shops, music and entertainments, or at the foot of the Eiffel Tower.

My late elder brother Mohamed and his wife Ragaa living in Surbiton, Surrey, had extended their warm hospitality during our visit to London where we toured the British Museum and saw the Rosetta Stone. That artifact provided the key for understanding the ancient Egyptian writings in hieroglyphs enabling Egyptologists to read the transcripts engraved on the walls of temples, graves, obelisks, clay pots and others. Mohamed took us around, explaining to our children the history the Tower of London, the Cathedrals, and the buildings of the British Parliament with the famous clock Big Ben.

We were also keen to show our children the United States, so that they could be proud not only of their parents' roots but of their own great country. They were already familiar with the East Coast, but when Arlene Sayegh, the wife of my good friend and mentor Fayez Sayegh, asked me to give away their daughter Reema at her wedding to Hal Lange, we seized the chance to show Yasmeen and Kareem a part of the country they had never seen: Las Vegas and the West. We flew from Washington to Los Angeles, and as we landed, I explained to them the history of the great metropolis. Unlike the skyscrapers of New York and Chicago, Los Angeles sprawls horizontally; no wonder the gasoline consumed in Los Angeles is the equivalent of that consumed by the entire country of France. We rented a car and saw the sights, from Universal Studios in Hollywood to Disneyland and San Diego, before driving on to Las Vegas. Las Vegas was intoxicating. Everything goes there: money, gambling, and sex. It was a sleepless human zoo. And it was a new city: In 1910, its total population was only 30 people. The casino hotel where we stayed was immense. Its entire lower floor was flooded by bright lights illuminating different types of gambling, from roulette to slot machines and many other devices. This was my first time in a casino, and although I saw some sporadic exultation as players won I saw much more disappointment, agony, and pain.

We later visited the Grand Canyon, Hoover Dam, Flagstaff, and the immense Meteor Crater at Winslow before driving back to California and up to San Francisco via the Pacific Coast Highway. On the way we visited the legendary Pebble Beach Resorts, between Monterey and Carmel with its world-renowned golf courses. The area and its streets were unbelievably clean. We noticed at that time signs reading "Littering $1000 Fine" strictly enforced by marked and unmarked police cars. The scenic road of Highway 1 West is undoubtedly the most beautiful coastline in the world. It was also frightening for Yasmeen, who observed the long fall over the side of the road down into the Pacific and told Kareem, "Stop talking and let dad concentrate on his driving!"

Upon arriving in San Francisco, we tried to find a place to stay but in vain. All hotels and motels were fully booked. We discovered that it was the time when the American Bar Association held its meetings. I remarked to my children, "This country is over-lawyered." It dawned on me to call the manager of the Fairmont

Hotel who had attended my presentation on petrodollars some fifteen years earlier before a large crowd of bankers, business executives, media and politicians in its ballroom. Following my speech, the hotel manager walked his way through the crowd around me to tell me how impressed he was by my perceptive analysis. He gave me his business card and asked me to let him know next time I came to San Francisco. I called him up and told him about our predicament. Upon checking, he informed me that that the only vacancy he had was a large two-room, two-bath suite with a reception area similar to that where Mrs. Jehan Sadat had stayed one week earlier. He gave it to me at the price of a regular room during our three-day stay. I appreciated his hospitality as he greeted us when we pulled at the front of the main entrance.

San Francisco was romantic and marvelous. I took the family on the usual tour of the city, from the Golden Gate Bridge to Fisherman's Wharf. We visited Alcatraz Island in the harbor and the redwood trees to the north of the city. It was a wonderful educational trip about the United States and its diversity.

As believers in Plato's theory of education, we introduced Yasmeen and Kareem to the world of sports, music, and the arts. They both played soccer, and Céline drove them regularly to private piano lessons and ballet school for Yasmeen, and kept after them to practice at home. It was unfortunate that Kareem tore a ligament in his right knee when he was ten years old that necessitated painful surgery at Georgetown University Hospital. Our good friend Galal Aref, an angel in disguise, was visiting us from Egypt. Being a professor of medicine himself, he sat next to his bed all night long holding Kareem's hand and giving him appropriate medication. He learned to walk using crutches, and he did surprisingly well in school despite spending two months healing and in physical therapy.

Kareem left his mark at that St. Albans School when he founded The Encore Club, and became its first president. When he was sixteen, he assembled a dedicated group, ages 14 to 18, from his school and the National Cathedral School for girls. At the very first concert of the Encore Club at St. Alban's Hearst Auditorium on November 22, 1996, Kareem welcomed the audience saying, "The Encore Club was established to contribute to charitable purposes by giving concerts to raise funds to help less privileged but gifted children who desire to learn classical music."

The story was admirably received amongst Céline's colleagues at Georgetown University's French Department. Roger Bensky gave Kareem great and constructive ideas. Aurelia Roman, originally from Romania, was able to locate a young musically gifted boy from a remote village in Transylvania, where allegedly Dracula came from. It was such a poor village that had only one telephone line.

Kareem wrote a letter to the well-known Interlochen Center for the Arts in Michigan seeking admission of Marius in the summer program. Having been impressed by the mission of the Encore Club, the Interlochen Center gave Marius a scholarship of $1,000. A close friend of mine, Mansour Hassan, came to dinner one evening during his visit to the United States. After Kareem gave a piano recital, he explained the mission of the Encore Club. Mansour, a top former aide to President Sadat, was moved by the idea and donated one thousand dollars.

At the Encore Club's concert on April 3, 1998, after thanking the audience for their continued support, Kareem announced: "It is my pleasure to inform you that Marius Copaceana, a young Romanian who won second place in the international competition in Romania, has been accepted at the Interlochen Center for the Arts in Michigan."

By hosting concerts, The Encore Club raised the money to pay for all expenses of Marius—even the cost of obtaining a visa to the United States. Before he traveled to Michigan, Marius was welcomed at our home enjoying an unforgettable taste of America. He spent hours in our backyard and swam in our pool. Kareem treated him as a young brother.

It was discovered that Marius did not have a French horn. After the purchase of his airline ticket and all other expenses, there were no funds available to purchase such an instrument that cost thousands of dollars. I related my concern to Mohamed Benaissa, the Moroccan ambassador to the United States. At a dinner at the Moroccan Embassy, Céline and I, as frequent invited guests, sat around a typical Moroccan round table. The Moroccans believe that there is always room for one more guest around a round table, a sign of welcome and generosity. At the dinner table, Mohamed talked about the Encore Club at St. Albans School. He also announced a piano recital after dinner given by Kareem and his own son, Amin, both of whom were seated at another table. Mrs. Silverman, a well-known New York philanthropist supporting the arts was moved by Kareem's dedicated efforts to bring in a musically gifted thirteen-year-old boy from faraway. She announced on the spot that she would donate the money for the expensive French horn for Marius. The Reverend Daniel R. Heichman, the faculty advisor to the En-core Club, purchased a St. Albans shirt for Marius. Even after Ka-reem's graduation in 1998, the Encore Club offered Marius another chance to come to the same program in 1999. The story was brought to the attention of the White House. President Clinton wrote a letter to Kareem on June 4, 1998, congratulating him on his mission. The letter said: "By using your talent and energy to help another de-serving young person reach his God-given potential, you represent America at its best."

In her senior year, Yasmeen volunteered to work as an unpaid intern at the White House receiving a memorable letter from Presi-dent Bill Clinton. In his senior year, Kareem devoted his time to helping poor kids in the inner city. He fulfilled his community ser-vice by working at the orthopedic department at Georgetown Uni-versity Hospital in gratitude for the medical care he received after his knee operation when he was in elementary school.

I was contacted in 1990 by Simon & Schuster to review a manu-script written by Thomas Hauser entitled *Muhammad Ali, His Life and Times*. Before it was to be published, the boxer insisted that the manuscript be read by a prominent scholar to make sure that nothing in it would give the wrong interpretation either of Islam or about him as a Muslim. I accepted the task, and was happy to find that Muhammad Ali was indeed (as I wrote) "a religious man who adheres to the principles of Islam and who is devoted to the wor-ship of God."

While the book was being printed, Muhammad Ali contacted me from Beirut asking me to respond to a narrow-minded cleric who showed him his displeasure for having allowed a Jewish au-thor to write his autobiography. It was a long telephone conversation. I used parts of the Holy Quran and the sayings of Prophet Muhammad to convince both the limited cleric and Muhammad Ali himself that there was nothing wrong to have a Jewish writer author the book. The boxer was impressed by how I had totally turned the cleric around.

Upon his return to his home in Michigan, he contacted me to thank me once again. He informed me that he would be traveling to Washington, D.C., and that he would like to visit me and my family at our home. The word quickly spread in our neighborhood and among Yasmeen's and Kareem's schoolmates that the famous boxer would be visiting us. None of us had ever seen him in person; we did not know how tall Muhammad Ali was. It was only when he entered the house one afternoon in November 1991 that we realized how big he was. My brother Zakaria next to him looked like a midget. We also discovered the great sense of humor of the Champ, as we all called him. He played magic to the amazement of the children present. He stood on one foot, concealing the other behind it, and in standing on the tiptoe of the unseen foot it looked as though he had lifted all of his body an inch or so defying the law of gravity. He asked Kareem to pretend he was giving him a blow at his nose. Muhammad Ali fell on one of our couches as though he received a knock-out blow.

When it was time for them to leave, he asked me to call a taxi. Again, we were surprised at his modesty for not coming in a limousine. I insisted in driving him to his hotel in Washington. On the way in and all along Connecticut Avenue, people in other cars recognized him and cheered the champ. Indeed, Muhammad Ali was one of the most famous people in the world. For a while, our children did not want to dispose of our 11-year-old Cadillac Seville because Muhammad Ali once sat in it.

The years of continuous driving slowed down somewhat when both Yasmeen and Kareem got their driver's license and particularly after they went to college. Yasmeen entered the College of Arts and Sciences at Georgetown University. She had a double major, English and psychology. Kareem was enrolled at Georgetown University School of Foreign Service majoring in culture and politics. They both lived in or close to campus. But occasionally they came home for a good meal and to attend to their laundry. Our live-in housekeeper Aicha had always been taking good care of them since we brought her from Morocco in 1992.

For several years, we were all at Georgetown University, meeting coincidentally in hallways or in elevators. Céline was in the French Department on the fourth floor, while I was in the Department of Economics on the fifth floor of the Inter Cultural Center, better known on campus as ICC Building. Our kids were actively moving from their classes to the various other activities on campus. It was a wonderful period.

The excitement of the graduation of Yasmeen and Kareem from Georgetown University lives forever in our minds. I was touched at the gesture of the University President John J. DeGioia when he asked me to give the diploma to Kareem while sitting with the other robed faculty on stage before the whole graduating class, families, friends and the large crowd in attendance. After graduation from college, both Yasmeen and Kareem got married and the family circle got larger—especially when Yasmeen delivered two adorable children, Ashling, born in November 2007, and her brother, Kieran, three years later.

In December 1992, when Yasmeen was 13 and Kareem was 12, I took the whole family for an overseas trip. We flew on the supersonic Concorde from Washington to London. In the first row, Yasmeen sat by the small tiny window of the Concorde next to her mother, while Kareem across a narrow corridor sat by the other window next to me. When we passed the sound barrier, we could not hear it as we were flying Mach 2, twice the speed of sound. I took them to the plane's cockpit where the pilots explained the sophisticated art of the field of aeronautics. The nose was straight as an arrow piercing its way through the skies. Since we were flying at the height of 60,000 feet, twice the level of a normal jet, we could see the curvature of the earth. It took less than four hours of flying before we arrived in London to be met by brother Mohamed.

We continued to Doha, but stopped on the way for seven hours to see the beautiful city of Manama. Farouk Almoahyyed, a prominent Bahraini, met us at the airport and planned the whole visit to capture the landmarks of his modern progressive country. I had an earlier encounter with his cousin Tarek Almoahyyed, Bahrain's

Minister of Information, whom I had invited for a conference in Washington. Following a quick lunch, our gracious host toured with us giving a bird's-eye view of his country.

From Manama, it was only a fifty-minute flight to Doha, where we were royally treated. For years, I had been an economic advisor writing occasional studies pertaining to the economics of oil and energy submitted to Issa Ghanem Al-Kawari, the chief of the Amiri Diwan. We had two suites overlooking the Arabian Gulf at the Doha Sheraton with its attractive pyramidal design. We visited one of the landmarks of the country that had significantly changed ever since it was gliding downhill on sand dunes. Before we arrived at the starting point, the driver stopped to deflate the four tires. From a high point, my children still remember the driver saying in English, "Hold your breath, fasten seat belts, no smoking, no talking," as he descended meticulously in a zigzagging fashion to avoid an unnecessary and dangerous acceleration. In fact, accidents do occur from time to time when an inexperienced or untrained driver is behind the steering wheel. At the foot of the high hill we descended, there was a tent with food and drinks facing a quiet beach just across from the Saudi Arabian border on the other side. Upon returning to the Sheraton, we had a superb dinner on the hotel's roof deck with a breathtaking view of the water.

From Qatar, we flew to Muscat, Oman, where my time was devoted to meetings of the founding members of Sultan Qaboos University College of Commerce and Economics. The Sultan's special envoy, Omar Zawawi, gave my wife and children an official car with a driver to show them the landmarks of Oman, in particular its famous Portuguese fortresses. Oman's more than 1060 miles of coastline provided the country with outstanding natural harbors. No wonder it has a long, diverse and far-reaching maritime history and great strategic importance. By the eighth century AD, Oman's ships reached ports in China allowing trade and intercultural connections with far corners of Asia. Islam was spread as people observed the practice of the pillars of the religion and the honesty—among other great values—of Muslim traders.

According to our travel itinerary, we took Saudi Airlines from Muscat to Riyadh in December 1992. In respect to Saudi traditions, both my wife and my thirteen-year old daughter wore black *abaya* and covered their hair before we landed. Members of the Saudi royal family extended the red carpet reception for us. Prince Fahd bin Khalid and his wife held a large dinner party at their palace in my honor. It was attended by his father Prince Khalid, his brothers Prince Salman, Prince Saoud, Prince Ahmed and his brother-in-law, my former student Prince Mohammed bin Nawaf, who later became the Saudi ambassador to the United Kingdom. The main reception area was built around a superb tall tree under a glass dome. He told us the story of a tree specialist advising his wife of the need to trim part of it before it could damage the dome. She refused, and instead asked the architect who built it to increase the height of the glass dome. The conversation was intellectually stimulating, as everyone spoke in impeccable English (they had all been educated in the United States). Yasmeen and Kareem had a ball with other children in the palace to the extent they asked to stay after we leave. Later a personal secretary brought them back all the way to the door of our suite at the hotel.

With the inflow of petrodollars following the quadrupling of the price of oil effective January 1, 1974, and being the country that possessed the largest known reserves of oil, Saudi Arabia embarked on an unprecedented development and urbanization programs. A world-renowned city planner told me that Saudi Arabia in the mid-1970s was a heaven for architects for they were not faced with financial constraints others typically encountered elsewhere in the world. Thanks to this largesse, the city is a gem. Each ministry has its own unique architectural design and shape.

Through its super network of wide well-designed streets and overflying bridges at intersections constructed with uniquely smoothed shapes, we went to visit Dereya, the original House of Saud of the royal family in the outskirts of Riyadh. Prince Mohamed bin Nawwaf told me he was born in this complex. It was all constructed with clay and natural raw material. It was where his grandfather King Abdul-Aziz and many of the royal family were born. King Abdul-Aziz Al-Saud became the first monarch of the Third Saudi State in 1932 after having spread his control over its entire current boundaries. We noticed the traces of some damages at Dereya caused by the 1813 bombardments of Ibrahim Pasha, the commander of the Egypt's army and the son of Mohamed Ali,

Egypt's ruler. It happened upon orders of Istanbul to invade Saudi Arabia, after having followed the teachings of the 18th century theologian Mohammed Abdel Wahhab and the dominance of the strict sect of Islam known as Wahhabism. Egypt, Mesopotamia and the entire Saudi Peninsula were then part of the Ottoman Empire.

From Riyadh we flew to Jeddah, the largest city in the kingdom. Saleh Seirafi and his entire family invited us to dinner where a whole roasted lamb was served in a gigantic covered silver decorated tray. Saleh started his business as a money exchanger in Mecca and grew significantly after having purchased large lots of land to be partly sold in millions of dollars with the surge of real estate prices. His wife is an Egyptian, not an uncommon practice in the eastern province of Saudi Arabia for three reasons. First, Egypt used to send Al-Mahmal every year with, Kiswa al-Sharifa, a new well-embroidered cover of the Kaaba, the holiest shrine of the Muslims, together with a gift of food and clothes at a time when the Saudis were poor and without resources. Second, there have traditionally been strong ties between their peoples particularly since the sixth century with geographical proximity of the two countries separated by the Red Sea. And third, Egypt used to send teachers for Saudi elementary and high schools at the expense of the budget of Egypt's Ministry of Education.

We had a tour of the traditional district of Jeddah that had been well restored with the Mesharrabias, wooden windows artistically decorated with small halls allowing those behind them to see the outside but not vice versa. The traditional *souk* Qabil within its narrow streets had diverse small shops selling gold, silver, rugs, colorful Indian and Chinese silk, cloth, fresh fruit and miscellaneous varieties of small items. Hamza took us to an old building owned by his father in the heart of old Jeddah; he could use his artistic talents to renovate it since his young brother Anas has set up an architectural design studio after his graduation from college in architecture. We passed by the National Commercial Bank, an impressively high modern building, owned by Salem Ben Mahfouz, a Saudi whose family came originally from Yemen. At its immense entrance, an old beaten-up wooden desk was placed under a glass dome. It was the desk that Mr. Salem Ben Mahfouz used in Mecca as a money exchanger, exactly the same as that of Saleh Seirafi, another wealthy merchant who became one of the top money exchangers in Saudi

Arabia. His last name means money exchanger, because some family names in the Arab world are derived from their professions. There was yet a third money exchanger, Al-Rajhei, who had also amassed huge wealth, opened a bank and invested in a variety of real estate out of the original money exchanging business for pilgrims coming from the furthest corners of the world.

The high point of our travels came when we were driven to Mecca to perform Umrah, same as the pilgrimage except that the latter has to be at a specific date of the Islamic calendar. At a gate before we arrived in the holy city, we had to show our identities as Muslims. A few years after our marriage Céline started to read the French translation of the Qu'ran by Régis Blachère. On her own initiative, she decided to become a Muslim by declaring that she testifies that there is no god but God and that Muhammad is his messenger. On my Egyptian passport, her picture was affixed as my wife near a notice that she became a Muslim before the Counselor Mohamed Issa at the Egyptian Embassy in Washington, D.C.

At the hotel in Jeddah, after ablution, we changed our clothes to wear Ihram, consisting of two long wide towels without stitches to cover a naked skin, one is to be securely wrapped around the waist all the way to the feet while the other is around the shoulders covering one shoulder and chest but allowing the other arm to be free. Upon coming close to Mecca, we saw the impressive minarets around the Kaaba. Having fulfilled the fifth pillar of Islam by going to the pilgrimage in 1990 and having performed the Umrah many times, I explained to my family its rituals. Prince Bandar bin Sultan, the Saudi ambassador to the United States, arranged for us to stay at the Royal Guest Palace overlooking the Kaaba.

Every time one satisfies human need, he or she must do the ablution by washing the hands and face, rinsing the mouth, cleaning the ears and nose, and washing the arms, hair and the neck as well as the feet. Other than Umrah, Muslims do the ablution five times a day before every prayer, the dawn, the noon, the early afternoon, the sunset and before bedtime prayers. Islam is a religion of purity and cleanliness. Having observed such features by others in India, Southeast Asia and elsewhere in addition to Muslim honesty and character as they moved along trading, people turned to Islam in substantial numbers without conquest or war.

After a short rest in our suite, we heard the call for the sunset prayer. We went down, crossed a street and walked a short distance to get in the mosque through Bab-el-Salam entrance, the Peace Entrance. Not only is Islam a derivation from peace but it in fact emphasizes it. Salam Alaikum means peace upon you. The four of us sat in the circles around the Kaaba where every worshipper faces it. Upon the second call for the prayer, we all stood to pray in utter humility hearing the Imam reciting Sourat Al-Fatiha followed by another Soura from the Holy Qu'ran before we bowed ninety degrees in respect to God the Great by repeating Sobhana Rabbia Al-Azeem three times. We stood after hearing the Imam saying "Allahu Akbar"—"God is the High"—and then kneeling to the floor with our heads touching the floor while saying and repeating three times Subhan Rabbia Al-Ala, praying to God the High. This is called one Rakaa, kneeling. The sunset prayer consists of three Rakaas. In the second Rakaa, we kept on our knees but with our chest and head up to read Al-Tahiyyat, including the testimony that there is no god but one God while lifting only one index finger as the indication of the oneness of God, praise be upon Him. The dawn prayer consists of two rakaas, the noon: four, the early afternoon: four, the sunset: three, and the prayer before bedtime: four. As we finished the prayer, Céline turned to me and said, "I have never thought I would be so moved as to the extent of feeling the hairs on my hands rise." Kareem was also deeply moved. "I wish I'd die in Mecca," he said.

Following the prayer, we started the Umrah by the *tawaf*, turning counterclockwise around the Kaaba seven times while reading from the small pamphlet we have in our hands, our prayers to God Almighty, ending with a kiss or a touch of the black stone and a prayer behind the tomb of Prophet Ibrahim, Abraham. According to Islamic tradition, the black stone at the eastern cornerstone of the Kaaba dates back from the time of Adam and Eve. If one cannot reach it because of the crowd, it is sufficient to point out to it with a raised hand. The black stone is smoothly polished because of the touches of an incalculable number of Muslims for many centuries. We flew to Medina to pray at the other Holy Mosque, Al-Masjid al-Nabawi, where Prophet Muhammad was buried. King Fahd's expansion was indeed a masterpiece in architectural design.

My family also included my siblings. In 1970, I lost one brother, Hassan, a chemist and a musician who loved to travel and was well versed in English, French, German, and Italian. He died at a young age after a period of personal depression following his last trip abroad and a failed love story. In 2006, I lost another brother, Yehia, who died at the age of 58 of diabetes and heart complications. My third brother, Mohamed, was four years older than I, and I had the strongest ties to him. When Nasser nationalized his business in the early 1960s, he and his family moved first to Nigeria, but in order to provide a good education for the children, they decided to immigrate to the United Kingdom in 1971. He became a British subject along with his wife Ragaa and his three sons, Yassin, Amr and Yehia and bought a house in Surbiton, Surrey, a suburb of London not far from Wimbledon.

Upon learning from his son Yehia and his wife Suzie on Wednesday, September 19, 2007, that my brother Mohammed in London had had a sudden stroke on his eightieth birthday, I took an all-night flight from Doha, where I had been teaching at the newly established branch of Georgetown University in Qatar since 2005. Upon arriving, I went to the hospital where my nephew informed me that his father had passed away one hour earlier. It was an opportunity to sit next to his body, as if he was sleeping. For an hour and half, I meditated and prayed for his soul while his three sons were making the necessary arrangements and the hospital paperwork was completed in preparation for the removal of his body. We accompanied him to a nearby mosque for prayer and for burial preparation, which took place shortly afterwards. His body was peacefully laid down in the ground on an eight by three foot grave under the shadows of majestic trees. The Islamic cemetery where he was buried amidst greenery on vast, serene grounds is not far from his home. His wife, three sons, their wives, two of his grandchildren and I received many people who came to his home until late in the evening. I spent Friday with his wife, Ragaa, and family.

After the prayer, we went to the cemetery to pray and pay my last respects to him. Mohamed was a good man, always remembered by his devotion to God and to his family, generosity, passion, care, kindness and good deeds. He was loved by all he had encountered in his life. My words "Life starts with a cry. Let it end with a smile" were quite applicable to his case. His wife informed me that when he felt some chest pain, he himself called an ambulance with a smile on his face, so that she thought he was joking. He lived in peace and died peacefully. On July 13, 2010, my eldest brother Youssef died at age 85. He was a prominent lawyer at Egypt's Supreme Court and had practiced law in nearby Alexandria for about fifty years until he retired. Before burial on the same day according to the Muslim tradition, his body was washed and wrapped in white cloth. A prayer was held and soon after he was carried by members of the family all the way to a graveyard where he was buried in the ground at the bottom of a dug out grave.

I have now one brother and four sisters all married with children and grandchildren. After the death of my two elder brothers, I became the dean of the Oweiss family.

It was early in the afternoon on August 15, 2001, when my 20-year old nephew Omar called me up.

"My mother is dead," he said. "I have just been released from police interrogation."

"What? What?" I replied in a mixture of shock and utter disbelief. "Where is your father?"

"He is in police custody," Omar replied.

"If you are permitted to drive your car, come right away to our home with your brother and your housemaid," I said.

Upon turning on our television set, we saw the house of my brother Zakaria in the posh neighborhood of Potomac, Maryland, cordoned off by a yellow ribbon, with several police cars, an ambulance, paramedics and a crowd outside. The media rushed to cover the tragedy. The evidence in favor of my brother Zakaria was dismissed on technicalities by a biased judge. At the exact time of the brutal death of his wife, my brother was not at home. He was paged and returned immediately to find his wife lying in a pool of blood. He asked his son to call the police. Paramedics were quickly on the scene. The basement's door to the garden was opened, but that was not recorded by police. A homicide investigator assured me that the hammer used in hitting my sister-in-law must have been carried by someone taller than her because of the angle of the hits as shown by medical autopsy. My brother was a few inches shorter than his wife, Marianne.

Throughout his trial, I got to respect only one lawyer, Nancy Luque, who was unfortunately unable to continue to defend my brother but was instrumental in his release on condition of staying at our home. He was allowed to go out for meetings with his lawyers or whenever he was called to court or other justifiable reasons. Between his release on bail and the sentencing, a span of one and half years, he stayed at our home along with his two dogs, a brown Irish setter called Thunder and a white fluffy one called Sparky. Even though I am allergic to dogs as their smell makes me sick, I accepted them when my wife saw how attached my brother was to them.

In my diaries, I wrote the following:

This day, the 22nd of April 2002, was the first day of the trial. I drove my brother and we both entered the ten-story building of Montgomery County Court House. After waiting in line for security, we deposited our bags in a conveyer. The keys, cell phones, loose coins, and anything else metallic were deposited on a separate tray. When I went trough the two-bar detector, there was a buzz. I was asked to lift my arms up while I was checked by a hand-held detector, then I was told to turn around in the same fashion. It was O.K. My brother as well as all others had to go through the same procedure.

In the large entrance hall, there was an information booth with a nice lady behind the counter. In the grim environment of the building she had a kind face with a faint smile. My brother asked her where was the hearing conducted by Judge Michael Pincus. She said, "Court Room number 4 on the 9th floor."

There were three other passengers in the elevator we took. One pushed 7, the other pushed 8 and my brother pushed 9. I was not in a hurry, but every time the elevator stopped, I looked up the number in utter silence, thinking of the fate that led us to a building we probably would have never entered.

Court Room number 4 has six seats on each side, four rows that can seat 24 persons in almost one third of the spacious high-ceiling courtroom. Facing us, the judge's high black chair is clearly visible between the U.S. flag and the flag of the State of Maryland. Below where the judge sits and immediately to his left sits the clerk in a semi circle configuration and two police officers. On the judge's right-hand side there is another lower level seat with a microphone for a witness stand. Facing the judge there is another semi-circle place for the defendants, prosecutors and jury if any.

On the ceiling there is a perfectly round light fixture with direct and indirect lighting.

"All rise."… We did, as the judge entered the spacious court room.

We repeated that trip, with the same frustrations and the same dehumanization, for eleven months.

Marianne's will named me the executor of her estate. Instead of leaving such a position to a law firm or other entity charging enormous amounts of money, I accepted it for free of charge in spite of the fact that I was informed that no executor of an estate carries such duties without fees. It was a challenge for me to follow the will of the deceased to the letter, to sell two properties, time-sharing for vacations, and her valuables. Since I retired from teaching at Georgetown University in 2002 at age 70, I devoted my time to helping my brother and his two sons as well as to attending to my duties as the executor of the estate of my sister-in-law for the benefit of her two sons. The efforts were monumental in the liquidation of all the assets until the task, demanding years of hard work and enormous efforts, was completed.

Two events created even more bias against him as a Muslim: the September 11 attack that was immediately perceived as the act of Muslim extremists, and a sniper that killed innocent people indiscriminately in shopping areas in both northern Virginia and Montgomery County in Maryland. The killer was a Black Muslim. In the selection of the jury for my brother's trial, a woman of Jewish descent told the judge as she pointed to my brother, "He is a suicide bomber killing my people." She referred to the Palestinians under the brutal occupation of their lands. Such incidents reflected the atmosphere of community bias, and hence my brother was not given a fair trial.

In spite of all the bias against my brother, the jury could not reach a conclusion and were hung for five days until they were told that he was willing to agree to a plea bargain. The fact of the matter is that two of his lawyers wanted to shove it down his throat by having him accept a plea bargain. He utterly refused.

Erin Uy, a reporter, described the scene at Zakaria's sentencing:

> More than 20 friends, family members and patients testified Friday [May 23, 2003] at the sentencing of Potomac gynecologist Zakaria M. Oweiss, who a jury convicted in February of his wife's second-degree murder in 2001. They described Oweiss, 59, as a devoted father, loving husband and dedicated doctor who cared for each baby he delivered. Celine Oweiss of Kensington, Oweiss's sister-in-law, implored for leniency in his sentence in order for him to be reunited with his family, "Give him the hope to be the same devoted and unlimited father and husband that he was," she said. But Circuit Court Judge S. Michael Pincus was not swayed. Although state guidelines recommended a 12 to 20-year sentence for such a crime, Pincus instead imposed the 30-year sentence.

A life and a family had been shattered. Yet the appeal looks promising for his release. He spends his time between his prayers and the assistance to those in need. In my periodic visits to him at the Maryland House of Correction where he had been detained, I found him to be spiritually strong in spite of his failing health and the complications of diabetes. I continue to support him utterly. I carried him as a baby on my shoulders when I was a teenager. I saw him crawling, walking, running and becoming the captain of his football team until I left him as a teenager when I departed to the United States early in 1960. In my first trip back to Egypt in 1970, Zakaria had just graduated from Alexandria University Medical School, and I managed to get him to the United States in 1972 to pass his examination given by the Educational Commission for Foreign Medical Graduates. He stayed with me during his years of residency and early years of his practice even after I got married. I believe in him and in his innocence. He is my brother.

To conclude this chapter of my marriage and raising the family, I thought of including the letter I wrote to Céline on our anniversary while I was away teaching in Qatar:

I could not believe how fast the year had rolled since I e-mailed you from Morocco on this wonderful occasion. Today is our 32nd wedding anniversary. As I grow older, the span of time between any two anniversaries seems to become shorter. I thought as if it was a month ago when I sat down to my computer to express my thoughts on this happy occasion last year. I was deeply touched by the response I received from Yasmeen, Kareem and Julie.

I hasten to send this message hoping that you open the Internet the first thing in the morning, of course after pan-caking, drinking your orange juice and sipping your coffee. Remember the wedding anniversary dinner prepared and served by Yasmeen and Kareem when they were very young, with candle lights. Yasmeen with a beautiful dress she chose for the occasion and Kareem with shirt and tie decided not to sit down with us, but to wait on us, serving one dish after the other, replacing plates, pouring drinks whenever they observed there was a need for more and taking pictures. They were so resourceful to prepare the dinner and to serve it eloquently and with love at a time in between two housekeepers, after we dismissed the young girl Laila for her jealously of Yasmeen and before the mature Aicha was hired.

I am delighted that you ended up marrying an economist to help you balance your budget. It was destiny to have brought you to the USA and to have lived in Arlington where our paths first crossed. It was then at Georgetown University we found out how suited we are for one anther. We were blessed to have Yasmeen, the devilish, who kept telling her friends at Stone Ridge School that she was a test-tube baby. It was after we invited Dr. Howard and Dr. Georgeanna Jones the pioneers in in-vitro fertilization along with Mrs. Sadat to our home. Yasmeen did not know at that time that the first baby in the United States ever to be born through in-vitro fertilization was Elizabeth Carr two years after Yasmeen was born.

Fifteen months later, a superb baby boy Kareem was almost born at the White House when President Carter invited us to a dinner in honor of President and Mrs. Sadat on April 12, 1980. When President Carter was looking at you and his eyes were fixed on your huge tummy, I directed my talk to him. "Thank you, Mr. President, for inviting the three of us." President Sadat had the biggest laugh; I wish I could find a recording of it. Do you remember when Kareem used two pacifiers in his infancy? When he was determined to quit both, we found him one morning not using either one. I wish he could use the same determination to quit smoking! Grandma had the best ending of her life amongst us caring for the grandchildren while becoming critical of you when she used to see you going out often for many social obligations. It prompted her to call you "Mademoiselle."

Remember the many honeymoons we had, particularly the one in Algeria, the other in Tokyo, Japan, and the third one we spent at the French Riviera staying in a suite at Hotel Martinez facing the water view and watching from our balcony the European nation's competition of breath-taking fireworks; our walk by the Croisette along with hundreds of other pedestrians in late afternoons after having meals served by the beach. Not to mention the awesome view of Petra in Jordan when we stood before another eternal colossus built by man. Do you remember our stay by the Dead Sea floating as small boats on its high-density salty water seeing Israel on the other side of the sea, or our spiritual visit to where Jesus was baptized and watching me pray at that site as I also did when we climbed up to the spot Moses had reached before he died at late age?

With all my travels, the Concorde years, you kept an eye on both children with utmost care, dedication, relentless efforts and unlimited love throughout their babyhood, growing years, sharing the continuous driving to schools, piano lessons, friends and too many other occasions, those physical efforts were replaced by mental worries when they started driving in their teens, teenage stage, years of college education and all the moving thereof, Kareem's demolishing two of our cars as total loss, Yasmeen's moving to New York, your decision to clean her windows to have a good view of the Empire State Building when you asked me to lift you on my shoulders, but inadvertently you sprayed Windex in my eyes while lifting you from below but I found soft warm place for protection, you know where!!, Kareem's falling in real love with Julie who brought happiness and eternal sunshine in his life and ours, his move to Crystal City at the job he got with the Africa Center for Strategic Studies on the day of his graduation from the university.

Remember Yasmeen's blessed meeting with Mark in New York made us all happy. Your excitement, I was afraid you would spill the drink at a restaurant when we took them out. You did! It was all over the table and the floor (a spill, the word you used in French throughout the years of our marriage, whenever we go out and being excited over the delicious plates you order, you scream "a spill" when you drop something on your beautiful clothes). Mark is a great fellow whom we grow to love immensely, the simple marriage of Kareem & Julie at the Arlington Court House on July 23, 2002, to be followed by another memorable occasion we are all waiting for on April 28, 2007 (I used to hate July 23 because it was the date of Nasser's revolution in 1952 that made Egypt stagnate for a while. Now I love that date because of Julie and Kareem), the eternally memorable and superb marriage of Yasmeen & Mark at the Four Seasons Hotel on September 10, 2005, with the unforgettable female bite on my hand following the religious wedding and on our way to the reception. From the doctor who treated me at Georgetown University Hospital, I learned that a human bite is worse than that of an animal. In my case it took a long time to heal.

Your teaching at Gonzaga, Sidwell Friends, and other institutions, with the longest tenure at Georgetown University, gained you all respect and admiration of your students and colleagues because of the devotion to your teaching throughout the years, even one student at Gonzaga had a crush on you. As the coordinator of French in Action, Kareem had initially designed your syllabus with a smiling face for holidays and sad faces for exams. Throughout the years, I was delighted to continue updating it for you.

When we moved temporarily to New York City, your role was so admirable while capturing the hearts and minds of those we encountered with your charming personality, cheerful face and meaningful conversations. You were a great hostess when we had people and friends at our home, the choice of the menus, the flowers, the table setting and the placement of our guests around the table were all done with exquisite taste. You made our home after we doubled its size and made other alterations over the years very homey and wonderfully furnished as your personality is felt everywhere: the plants at the entrance, the hanging paintings, the Persian rugs the majority of which we bought from specialized stores or auctions (remember when you kept elbowing me to out auction others for the unique and huge Persian rug that killed me to pay for it), antique furniture you brought from your mother's home in Belgium including a superb piano with its original gold mark that we had to sell as it was impossible to find the tools or the artisans to have it tuned, instead we kept upgrading the pianos until I made it a surprise when you came home one day to see a grand Steinway autographed by a grandson of Steinway replacing a Yamaha to suit the progress shown by our gifted children, the design of the entire area around the fire place with Italian mosaic that has an oriental touch, added pieces of furniture some of which from auctions, the many plants in our Florida room that Aicha keeps watering ever since we hired her.

The panorama of our 32 years of marriage is deeply embedded in my heart and soul. One can only portray selected glimpses of home or travels. Remember the cruises on the Nile River we did several times to visit the glory of the great Egyptian history from the Pharaonic times, Greco-Roman, Coptic to an Islamic center for knowledge, education, architecture.

Your support to Zakaria will never be forgotten following the family tragedy and your welcome to him and his dogs in spite of my opposition and my vomiting when I entered our home because of the filthy smell for almost one and half years between his release from detention until he was condemned harshly to prison for thirty years. Remember that you argued strongly for keeping the dogs for Zakaria's morale as he found in them great emotional support than what he got from his own two sons. I have hated dogs immensely ever since. When I visited Amr and Aouatif in Rabat where they have three dogs, they were all kept outside of the house and not allowed to enter under any circumstances. Nevertheless, I stayed with them in their beautiful home and with their lovely teen-age twin daughters Kenza and Dina for only two weeks rather than the full month. You chose to remember the days when he thought the world of you and his argument with me encouraging me to marry you. You opted to forgive him when he turned against you under the influence of his jealous wife and probably the emotional change inside himself against you. Amal Ghorbal once told me before she became seriously ill, "no woman ever can do what Céline did towards your brother Zakaria." You gained my admiration and love to you because of YOU.

You remember the several black-tie dinners we had for dignitaries, whether at home in Kensington or in New York City, the preparation under your meticulous supervision of each, the choice of flowers, the elegance of table settings and the artistic presentation is a story told in the many pictures now well classified in albums displayed on our shelves, some of which you chose to display in frames placed on the grand piano, bay windows or otherwise hanging on our walls.

Women are usually grouchy when they wake up in the morning without make-up, but ever since I met you, you are always beautiful, smiling, cheerful, eternally young (you definitely do not look your age), always enthusiastic and forgiving. In all of the 32 years of our marriage, I do not remember difficulties that we sometimes had faced. It was probably your forgiving nature as well as mine that we live happily together engulfed by the love of Yasmeen, Kareem, Julia and Mark while blessed by the enlarged families of the Whites, the Burns, their relatives and friends. We are indeed fortunate.

I noticed over the years since Sabry, the son of our house-keeper was born on March 20, 1995, how attentive you have always been to his education since his divorced mother had never attended school in her native country, Morocco, in spite of the fact she is notably intelligent, and hence could not assist him in the rigorous program you laid out for him to have a good education. I have always admired your re-lentless efforts to sit with the boy 3 to 4 hours every day to go over his homework and the way you directed him to play music, to participate in competition as you are prepar-ing his file to go to college.

I seldom say it because I have always acted to portray my affection in deeds not in words, but I wanted you to know that I love you. I feel now that it is "mission accom-plished," using your mother's last words. If I drop dead any time, I wanted you to know how I feel towards you. Do not forget what I always say: *life is for the living.* Enjoy life after me as you had always done ever since we met.

Love, Papa

Doha on July 19, 2007

Photo Gallery

With Ali Selim, aged seven. His parents Mo and Evelyn, his brother Ramy, and his sister Mona visited me in Washington, D.C., on their tour of the East Coast in 1969. Ali has become a renowned film producer in Hollywood. In 2005, his film *Sweet Land* won national and international prizes.

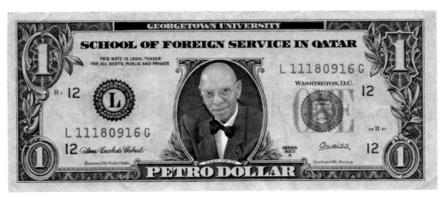

A "petrodollar" commissioned by the School of Foreign Service in Qatar and presented to me by Professor Amira Sonbol on May 8, 2009.

90

At an official ceremony in January 1978 with Ambassador Ashraf Ghorbal, standing between Secretary and Mrs. J. William Middendorf II. Céline and I are on his left. President Anwar Sadat awarded Secretary Middendorf and me the Egyptian Merit Decoration First Order.

Displaying my decoration at the Egyptian Embassy with Céline and Dr. Ashraf Ghorbal, Egypt's Ambassador to the United States.

Shaking hands with King Fahd and Prince Faisal in Riyadh, Saudi Arabia, at the Royal Palace in 1989.

A meeting with President Sadat in Cairo in 1980. President Anwar Sadat greets Dr. Armand Hammer, the Chairman of Occidental Oil Company, while Senator Albert Gore, Sr. looks on. I am explaining the project I am proud to have brought to Egypt to then-Vice President Hosni Mubarak, who does not seem to comprehend its scope or importance. The photo was taken after President Sadat's enthusiastic approval of the project.

With Céline and UN Secretary-General Boutros-Boutros Ghali at George-town University in 1993.

My wife Céline Marie-Joseph Lesuisse when we met in 1974.

With Céline on our wedding day, July 19, 1975.

Upon my appointment as Chief of the Egyptian Economic Mission to the United States with the rank of Ambassador at my office in New York in 1977.

My 22-month-old daughter Yasmeen kissing her brother Kareem, then only seven months old.

A family portrait from the 1980s.

Yasmeen at age 9 and Kareem at age 8 gave a piano recital at our home in honor of Mrs. Jehan Sadat in 1988. In the background is one of the paintings we bought from the famous Egyptian artist, Seif Wanley.

Kareem spars with Muhammad Ali in our living room.

With two of our grandchildren at Céline's seventieth birthday in 2010.

Sheikha Mozah received Céline and me at her private mansion on May 5, 2009.

To Dr. Ibrahim Oweiss
With best wishes, + Thanks   Bill Clinton

With President Clinton in the White House in 2000.

BILL CLINTON

Thanks so much for your support and encouragement.

With your help, we can change our country and put our people first.

Bill

A note from my most distinguished student.

With Queen Noor of Jordan during her visit to the Jones Institute.

At the CCAS inauguration on September 2, 1974. Clockwise from left: Senator J. William Fulbright, Ambassador Ashraf Ghorbal, me, Georgetown President Father Henle, Ambassador Saeed Ghobash, Minister Seif Ghobash, Dean Peter F. Krogh, and Professor Hisham Sharabi.

As the Chairman of Faith & Hope USA in 1976, after announcing its creation, I introduced (to my left) Mrs. Jehan Sadat, President Sadat's wife, Ambassador Ashraf Ghorbal, Actor Omar Sharif, Mrs. Ismail Fahmy (wife of Egypt's Foreign Minister) at The Egyptian Embassy in Washington DC.

With Mr. Juma Al-Majid from Dubai, a great philanthropist, who built four schools paying all educational expenses since their start in 1983. He also built the College of Islamic and Arab Studies in Dubai offering graduate degrees and a 55-million dollar library at his own expense to preserve original manuscripts, books, and rare maps he had personally purchased. It became a research center for scholars from all over the world, to which I donated my personal library collected over my life span.

At our home in 1996 with Crown Prince of Spain Prince Felipe during his
studies For Masters Degrees in Foreign Service, Georgetown University.
King Juan Carlos and Queen Sophia attended their son's graduation.

With His Highness Sheikh Khalifa Ben Hamad Al-Thani, the Emir of
Qatar, in 1993.

With President Anwar al-Sadat at Blair House in Washington, D.C., in August 1981.

Following a summit meeting with President Reagan in Washington, D.C., President Anwar Sadat received an honorary degree just six weeks before he was assassinated on October 6, 1981 in Cairo. I read the citation while President Sadat and Georgetown University's president, Father Timothy Healy, were standing on my right. Two months after the event, Father Healy held a full mass at Georgetown University's Dahlgren Chapel in honor of the brave head of state who had initiated peace with Israel as a first step for a comprehensive Middle East peace.

The last senior seminar I taught, ending 48 years of teaching at higher institutions of learning in the United States. On the right of my wife in the first row: Lina Abduljawad, AlJazi Darwish, Lubna Kayyali, Moham-med Al Attiyeh; on my left: Asma Al-Adawi, Safia Al-Naimi, Mashail Al-Naimi, Nicholas Nassar; second row: Ibrahim AlDerbasti, Sheikh Abdulla Hamad Al-Thani, Louloua Al-Rodaini, Mark Saliba, Basil Mahfouz, and Khalid Al-Jufairi.

3

Georgetown

I arrived in Washington the day before my lease began, and so I headed towards Georgetown Inn at the intersection of Wisconsin and M Streets northwest a few blocks away from Georgetown campus. It was after midnight when I pulled in the hotel's back garage. The clerk at the desk, well-dressed in a smart hotel uniform with several shining buttons on the jacket, greeted me warmly. "Welcome to Georgetown Inn. Please fill in this form," he said. "We have a room for you on the third floor. There is a recorded history for each room showing the celebrities that stayed in them at different times. Do you want to know who slept in the bed of the room I gave you?"

"No, thank you," I replied tiredly. But he kept going anyway as he handed me the room key.

"On that bed, Doris Day, Gregory Peck, Senator Dirksen, Hubert Humphrey…"

"Wait," I said. "Did you say Hubert Humphrey? Please give me another room."

I had lost my respect for Humphrey after I had heard him announce his candidacy for the presidency in a speech at the University of Minnesota Northrop Auditorium before my departure from Minneapolis. He spoke for about one hour amongst cheers, balloons and circus-type noise. He tried to please everyone, every school of thought, every minority, every majority, and every movement regardless of to whether or not they directly opposed one another. He ended up saying nothing of substance. Moreover, I had a personal feeling against him in spite of his continuous smile, cheerful face, some of his good record at the Senate for his stand for civil rights and his phenomenal memory in remembering names and faces even after meeting them only once. When I was president of the Arab-American Club in Minneapolis, I invited him to speak. He never answered. I ran into him once flying from Washington to Minneapolis. Luckily, his seat was next to mine. As he remembered my name, it was a good opening to renew my invitation for him to speak before an Arab-American group. He tried to get out by saying that he was pro-Israel. I argued that it would be useful for him to listen to another side. He promised to do it, but after we parted he chose to ignore his promise.

I moved into Arlington Towers just across the Potomac from Georgetown University at 1021 Arlington Boulevard, my address from September 1967 until I bought a house in Kensington, Maryland, when I got married in July 1975. It was an immense compound of rusty red brick buildings. There were four towers, each named after a former President of the United States from Virginia. Madison and Tyler were at the entrance of the complex while Washington and Jefferson were in the back facing the Potomac River. I rented apartment 1021, a one-bedroom suite with an immense living room, part of which was to be used as a dining area, a well-equipped kitchen, a full bathroom, and a large bedroom. From both the living room and bedroom, there was a wall-to-wall window giving a breathtaking panoramic view to the east and the southeast. Across the Potomac River were the immortal Egyptian-Greco columns of the Lincoln Monument, the Egyptian obelisk shape of the Washington Memorial, and the Capitol Building. To the southeast, one could see the tidal basin surrounded by attractive cherry trees, a gift from Japan, and what remains in my opinion the most beautiful of all monuments, the Jefferson Monument with its domed roof.

It took a while to unpack and put everything in order, as it had become my habit ever since I arrived in the United States to be meticulously organized. Such a habit takes time at the beginning, but it saves time from there on.

Georgetown University's Department of Economics was not inside the gate of the walled campus, but one block away on N and 36th Streets in the Nevils Building adjacent to the Walsh Building, with its landmark of a huge globe of the world. The Walsh Building was

named after Father Walsh, who started the School of Foreign Service in 1919 to educate young men in the fields of international relations. At that time, Georgetown University was not a co-education-
al institution of higher learning, but its School of Foreign Service
allowed women to enroll, before the College of Arts and Sciences
followed the same policy one year after I joined the University. In
fact, I taught at the College of Arts and Sciences to an all-male senior class in the fall of 1967.

Henry Briefs, the chairman of the department of economics
greeted me warmly from behind his desk with his typical pipe
sticking out from the corner of his mouth. Had he not been tall,
I would have probably not seen him sitting behind his desk, as it
was full of papers, books and files. He took me around to meet his
father, Professor Götz Briefs, who was 78 years old in 1967 but was
still working on economic philosophy. I was fortunate to have him
as a colleague for seven years.

We went to the office of Bruce Davie, a Harvard man, sitting
with Bruce Duncombe, who was a colleague of mine at the University of Minnesota. They were finishing their last revisions of their
book on public finance. Bruce Davie did not stay long at Georgetown University after he had set up and directed the Office of Institutional Research. He joined the economic policy division of the
U.S. Office of Management and Budget before he moved to the
Capitol as the chief tax economist with the House Ways and Means
Committee and then the Treasury's Office of Tax Analysis. Bruce
Duncombe decided to join the Foreign Service and became an economic counselor.

There was also a phenomenal Austrian economist, Josef Solterer, almost the same age as Professor Götz Briefs, with his thick
golden eyebrows. He was an authority on Joseph Schumpeter who
left his mark on the field of economics. Professor Solterer was a
former department chairman and had been a professor since the
1930s. He was a compatriot of giant thinkers in the field of economics including John Maynard Keynes, Gottfried Haberler, Ludwig
Von Mises and many others including, of course, Joseph Schumpeter.

Our chairman at the University of Minnesota, Jo Simler, had
informed me that he was a student of Josef Solterer when he finished

his military service after World War II. At that time, there were two groups of students, the first included those who had just finished high school and were admitted to Georgetown University, while the second was an older group who could not go to college right away because of the war but were given a chance to do their university studies afterwards. On a warm day with no air-conditioning, some of the older group dared to loosen their neckties and take off their jackets. When Professor Solterer entered the classroom, he ordered students to tie their neckties and wear their jackets, saying, "The British ruled hot India for a long time with their full attire on."

The chairman took me to meet another senior professor, Lev Dobriansky. Though he had a shining bald head, he had always been well tanned and handsomely dressed. He was of Ukrainian origin and had organized a group of the descendants of their ancestors in the Ukraine demanding independence from the Soviet Union. Lev was staunchly anti-communist and was the head of several right wing groups. Henry Briefs mentioned to me that a great colleague, Joseph L. Tryon, a Harvard man, would be returning to teach the following year. His areas of interest were international economics and economic development. Upon his return, we hit it well together. He later became the chairman after Henry Briefs.

We passed by the office of George Viksnins, originally from Latvia. He too was anti-communist in every respect. George had a distinctively big bearded face. His laughter could be heard from afar and his sense of humor would make a whole regiment crack with laughter. One time, I invited him to a Halloween party at my apartment. He chose to wear an Arab costume I had in the apartment. Then he went out knocking on my neighbors' doors with a hat in his hand saying he was collecting money for the United Jewish Appeal. His wife Mara and he held unforgettable New Year's parties at their town house on T Street within a few blocks away from campus.

I also met Bill Dinkelacker while rushing from a statistical lab to his office with a grim face as if he was carrying the world's problems on his shoulders. He gave the wrong impression about himself at a first meeting. When I got to know him, I found him to have a heart of gold, and to be a cooperative and genuine friend. He told me that there were others still to meet among the young professors,

William McElroy who was on leave in 1967-68, Ed Murphy and Donald Wood, who were both on a trip soon to return. Don Wood's father, a sea lover, invited his son Don, his daughter-in-law Karen and Tom Murphy to sail on his medium-size sailboat during the latter part of the summer from the west coast all the way to Hawaii. It was quite an adventure that the three of them upon return were talking about. Don Wood was a bright economic statistician who did not stay long in teaching. He was attracted to work with the Bureau of Labor Statistics to design and publish periodically the U.S. consumer price index, an indispensable tool used by economic researchers in the United States and elsewhere.

Ed Murphy, a descendant of President John Quincy Adams, was an international economist, tall, thin and dignified with a subtle sense of humor. He used to describe Bill Dinkelacker's grim look, "When Bill tells you that the weather is bad, he makes you feel as if you are responsible about it." After Bill had several accidents in his red Corvette whether on the road or simply being parked, he described him as "crash." Since both of us were among the younger generation, we socialized frequently and became friends for life.

At the end of the corridor where my office was located, before the steps leading to the Walsh building, there was a serious-looking hunchbacked professor, Cyril Zebot, originally from Croatia. I was touched by his kindness which I had felt immediately from our first encounter. He invited me to a party to be held at his home a week later. It was from him that I learned of what he had correctly predicted of the devastating ethnic cleansing by the Serbs once the communist dictator Tito was gone.

I was introduced to Father Joseph Zyrini, S.J., with his red round cheeks and serious look while he was on his way to a committee meeting. He invited me to have lunch with him at the campus ministry where superb food and excellent wine were served. Father Zyrini was a well-organized and dedicated teacher. Once, he was asked if a grade of one of his students could be modified. His answer became legendary: "Even if God asked me to change a grade, I would not do it."

Next to me was the office of Jeane J. Kirkpatrick from the Government Department. While next door to me for fourteen years, I discussed with her the problems of the Middle East. She held a pro-Israeli position, right or wrong, and refused to be enlightened by another point of view. She was envious of me when in 1977 I took a leave of absence from Georgetown University to assume my position as the chief of the Egyptian Economic Mission to the United States with a rank of ambassador. She did not dream that she would ever rise to such heights. Ironically, after reading an article she wrote, President Ronald Reagan chose her in 1981 to be the U.S. ambassador to the United Nations.

In other departments, I got to know prominent colleagues including Carroll Quigley, Hisham Sharaby and Jack Ruedy. In the Arabic Department, I met a remarkable sociologist, Riad El-Ani, and a prominent scholar in Byzantine studies, Erfan Shahid, and the kind, soft-spoken Wallace Erwin, who was the Department's chairman. Keith Fort, a tall thin professor of English, and I hit it well together once we got to know that we were both from the University of Minnesota. He was a good tennis player and had patience to play with me even though he was better than I. At the luncheon faculty room, we used to chat about literature and poetry, subjects close to my heart. I recommended to him to make arrangements to bring in Roland Flint, a sensitive poet, from Minnesota. Roland and I met at a class I was attending not for credit, but for the enjoyment of listening to John Orley Allen Tate with his kind smile, thin face, small moustache, big wide forehead and a penetrating voice giving imagery to what he recited from his own poetry or from that of others, including T. S. Elliott. Following his class, Roland and I used to comment about the inspiration Allen Tate had instilled in our hearts and minds. Through my introduction and the instrumental efforts of Keith Fort, Roland Flint was offered a position in the English Department. He became a colleague at Georgetown University and a friend for life until he died in 2001. Roland was a nationally recognized poet who was named poet laureate of Maryland.

It was after the University of Minnesota, another culturally stimulating environment, that I joined Georgetown University in 1967. Throughout the years of teaching, writing, contributions to my field, traveling, attending conferences, consulting, institutional building, and my diplomatic service while I was on leave from teaching, I gained a wide array of experience which I often brought to the classroom to the benefit of my students, before my first retirement from Georgetown University in 2002.

My commitment to activism did not lapse because I had joined the ranks of the faculty. At the time, the Vietnam War was raging. I lived through its trauma and had witnessed how the American society was deeply torn between the establishment calling for a continuation of the war until victory over North Vietnam, and an increasing majority, representing mainly the youth, against it. The United States first entered the war in 1950 in an attempt to prevent a communist takeover of South Vietnam, but the heavy involvement occurred in the nineteen sixties and hence causalities kept mounting. Every evening, television anchorman Walter Cronkite used to tally the death toll on each side.

I walked in the senior class at Georgetown University in which William Jefferson Clinton was enrolled and saw dispirited young men who knew that they might be drafted and killed in Vietnam. Among those killed was one of our brightest students, Joseph Mark Lauinger. His wealthy family, who owned *Oil and Gas Journal*, donated money to Georgetown University to build a badly needed library, which was then named in his memory.

In addition to teaching economics, I found my role to be consoling the young students and instill in them hope rather than despair. I talked to them not only in teaching at Georgetown University but also at youth gatherings in public places and sometimes in the basements of private homes. Teach-ins were one of the healthy outlets to express one's thoughts, to debate, to hear other points of view, to learn and comfort one another.

There were other forms of escape when some indulged themselves in drinking, smoking pot and taking drugs. The hippie movement was easily recognized by the young men's long hair, and the prevailing saying "never trust anyone over thirty" became a philosophy of most young Americans. The whole nation became aware of what was happening on campuses such as that of the University of California in Berkeley. Some young people got driven down a road of hedonism seeking nothing but pleasure and breaking traditions and sometimes laws.

One day I was contacted by some former students of mine at the University of Minnesota, who were among the organizers of the peace demonstrations planning their trip to Washington, to find a shelter for those coming in buses and private cars. The demonstrations in Washington were organized by "MOBE," the National Mobilization Committee to End the War in Vietnam. It comprised more than 150 different groups with some planned events for a single weekend in Washington.

I offered my place and helped to open the gym at Georgetown University. I even went to some churches in my neighborhood and schools to help out. In my apartment, I took in fifteen students, both graduate and undergraduate as well as one child. They were all thrilled by the panoramic view. Judy Andersen from Minneapolis shouted, "This is a place of peace, beauty and love…Let us put an end to the war." Until late they sang, recited poetry, played on the guitar, laughed and talked and talked as if there was no end to it. At night, there were bodies sleeping on the floor, on the couch, in the long balcony, in sleeping bags, on rugs, or otherwise on the floor. The kid and his parents shared my queen-size bed. In the morning, while trying to find a spot for my feet to walk amongst the sleeping bodies, I went to buy some eggs for breakfast, juice, paper plates, cups and all that I needed to feed the army I had in my apartment. I called on a friend of mine to come help, as I was not yet married. She and I managed to serve them breakfast in preparation for a long day of demonstrations.

As a believer in their cause, I joined them as we walked a long way crossing the Roosevelt Bridge to join the big crowds coming from all over the country. Among the speakers was Senator Eugene McCarthy whom I got to know, his daughter Ellen, who became one of my students, Dr. Benjamin Spock, the famous pediatrician whose book was on the shelves of every family, and many other peace activists. Dr. Spock aroused the crowds, "This war has been killing my children."

The three-day peace activities were full of true fraternity, soul searching and hope to end the meaningless war. As I bade farewell to all of my guests, some of whom I had never come across again while others kept in touch with cards and telephone calls, I told them that wars are incompatible with humanity. Have we learned our lesson? I guess not.

Another incident during my teaching days stands out. This is my diary from September 21, 1976:

I was almost killed or at least injured this morning. On my way to Georgetown University, I took a different route than what I regularly used. A thought crossed my mind after fifteen minutes of driving and on the spur of the moment, I changed my direction after I crossed Chevy Chase Circle at the borderline between Washington and the State of Maryland. Instead of going south on Wisconsin Avenue, I changed my direction as I decided to stop by the residency of the ambassador of Egypt, Ashraf Ghorbal, to agree on a mutually convenient time for a presentation I asked him to make at Georgetown University. I took Massachusetts Avenue south. Just before Sheridan Circle, a car passed me on my left. I gave it a chance to go ahead of me as I was not in a hurry and it has always been my nature to be courteous in my driving. I drove slowly as I entered into the circle.

The same car that passed me was about fifty feet ahead of me after it had just passed the intersection of the 24th Street northwest where the residency of the Turkish ambassador is located, a thunderous explosion blasted. I managed to stop immediately. Before my own eyes I saw a dreadful scene I shall never forget as if it was a part of the most horrifying movie one can ever see. I noticed the car doors blown out while a human leg was partially hanging out in the street. In a few minutes, sirens of police cars, ambulances and rescue squads were loudly heard while television and other media cars with their mounted cameras appeared quickly on the scene. A crowd started to form from afar as the police prevented pedestrians to come nearby. On my left, I noticed Ambassador Ghorbal rushing out from the large black doors of his residency running towards the back where his chancery was located on Decatur Place. He told later that he was in a hurry to find out what had happened and whether the bomb or bombs were to be directed towards either the residency of the Romanian ambassador or that of the Turkish ambassador.

As it turned out, it was a political assassination. A former Chilean minister of foreign affairs, Marcos Orlando Letelier del Solar, was killed by a bomb ignited by a remote control from afar only sixteen days after he was deprived of his Chilean citizenship. The Chilean DINA agents carried out the plan of assassination in daylight.

I encountered Letelier in 1971 at a conference and found him to be a colorful Chilean ambassador to the United States. We hit it well together as we were both economists, but we were of different economic orientations. Soon he was recalled by President Allende to serve successfully as the minister of Foreign Affairs, Interior and Defense. He was the highest-ranking official to be imprisoned and tortured following the September 11, 1973, overthrow of the Allende regime. Chile was then ruled by the dictator Augusto Pinochet and his military regime.

Upon recommendation from Diego Arria, then Governor of the city of Caracas in Venezuela, he was released on condition that he would immediately leave Chile. Obviously he went first to Caracas, but in 1975 he decided to move and reside in Washington. He became a senior fellow with the Institute for Policy Studies and taught at American University. Letelier became heavily involved in writing and speaking against the dictatorship of Pinochet and his military regime.

I am proud to have been one of the founders of Georgetown University Center for Contemporary Arab Studies, which became a world-renowned institution in its own right. Elias Shoufani joined Georgetown University in 1967 after having completed his doctoral degree at Princeton University under the supervision of an icon in the history of Islamic-Arab studies and the father of Middle East studies in America, Philip Khuri Hitti. He was an Israeli Arab well versed in Hebrew and a dedicated activist. Even though he was instrumental in bringing an idea to establish a center for Arab Studies at Georgetown University, he decided a year later to reside in Lebanon to join the struggle for the Palestinian cause. Yet his idea persisted. An ad hoc committee consisting of Hisham Sharabi, Elias Shoufani, and me held several discussions. We thought there was a need for establishing a contemporary Arab studies program at Georgetown University since Centers for Middle Eastern Studies in several universities in the United States usually shy away from involvement in contemporary issues except on some rare occasions.

We thought that we had the following assets as later published in the Center's first annual report:

> Georgetown University was the oldest and largest school of international relations in the United States.
>
> Tenured faculty members at Georgetown University could be a strong nucleus for the establishment of a Center for Contemporary Arab Studies.
>
> Georgetown University library possessed one of the largest Arabic language collections in the United States. In addition, Georgetown University is close to the nation's largest collections of books and manuscripts at the Library of Congress.
>
> A location in the capital of the United States provides ready access to invaluable resources of the governmental, diplomatic and private foreign affairs communities.

It took a few years before the idea turned into a course of action. In the early 1970s, we presented our vision to a newly appointed and dynamic Dean of the School of Foreign Service, Peter Krogh, who became enthusiastic about it and a great supporter. Clovis Maksoud, who was an adjunct professor for one year at Georgetown University, and Michael Hudson, who was on sabbatical from the Johns Hopkins University School of Advanced International Studies, joined our efforts. We formed a committee which John Ruedy, a professor of history, and Wallace Erwin, the chairman of the Department of Arabic, also joined. We invited Ambassador Ashraf Ghorbal to lunch at the office of the president of Georgetown University. He gave us new ideas for implementation. In his own visionary way, he concluded the meeting by saying: "Think big." We certainly did.

We had many advantages. Although we lacked money, we had the ingredients of an outstanding educational institution, tenured and accomplished faculty members, backing from the young energetic and resourceful dean Peter Krogh, and dedicated members of our committee. And so in 1975 when I learned of the official visit of Sultan Qaboos of Oman to Washington, I had lunch with the first Omani ambassador to the United States, Ahmed Makki. I asked him if the Sultan could give the seed money for the establishment of Georgetown University Center for Contemporary Arab Studies (CCAS) on the occasion of his visit. Ahmed Makki was a close friend of mine. Our relationship continued even after he had returned to Oman to assume first the position of Minister of Labor and Human Resources and then the Deputy Prime Minister for Economic and Financial Affairs. The gift of $150,000 was approved by the Sultan. A check was handed over to me. When I rushed with the good news to see Peter Krogh, he decided on the spur of the moment to launch the opening of the CCAS at a celebration during the World Bank–International Monetary Fund meetings held that year in Washington, an opportunity when ministers of finance and economics as well as central bankers of member countries congregate.

According to the Center's First Report, its purposes were set forth as follows:

> To improve the knowledge of students at Georgetown University about the contemporary Arab world.
>
> To undertake studies and issue publications addressed to contemporary problems and prospects in the field of Arab development and international relations with emphasis on Arab/American relations.
>
> To conduct public affairs activities directed toward improving official and public knowledge of Arab/American relations and the perspectives, interests and policies of the Arab world.
>
> To provide such technical assistance and consulting services as are consistent with the Center's resources and priority commitments with the priority commitments to teaching, research and publication.

Under the Chairmanship of Dean Peter F. Krogh, an Executive Committee was the principal policy making body of the Center for Contemporary Arab Studies. The Center's first Executive Committee was composed of Wallace Erwin, Michael C. Hudson, Dean Peter F. Krogh, David Long (Secretary), John Ruedy, Hisham Sharabi, and myself. John Ruedy was the first Chairman of the Program of Contemporary Arab studies who had skillfully designed a renowned two-year program leading to a Masters Degree in Arab Studies. I was the director of the Center's Institute of Arab Development and International Relations. In this capacity, I ran the Center's research, publications, public affairs and an annual symposium.

With his visionary outlook and dynamism, Dean Krogh formed an advisory board of American and Arab dignitaries. Chairman of the Board of the Royal Jordanian Airlines Alia Aly Ghandour was elected as the first Chairman of the Center's Board of Advisors. Former Senator J. William Fulbright had been a great supporter of the Center ever since it was established until he died.

Ever since the Center's creation, it has been subject to continuous and vicious attacks from all those who wish to have neither an objective study of the Arab world nor to reveal the historical truth about the Arab-Israeli conflict. It was less than four months after the CCAS was inaugurated when I was asked to have a meeting with Reverend Robert Henle, S.J., the president of Georgetown University at his office.

"Look, Dr. Oweiss, at the three large boxes in front of you," he said. "They include letters attacking me for having allowed CCAS to be established at Georgetown University. Some of them threatened to withdraw their financial and other support they had rendered in the past."

"Father Henle," I replied, "on many occasions ever since the CCAS was established, I heard nothing but admiration for your support of it and for your courage to fully endorse it. The time you allocate to reply to every single letter will be at the expense of the valuable time you are devoting for this great institution."

"What do you advise me to do?" he asked.

"I would recommend a short reply, the same letter to every one," I said. "'We have Soviet studies and Chinese studies centers, among others. So why not an Arab studies center?' If you receive follow up correspondence, it will be a pleasure to assist in your reply."

The recommendation worked. Father Henle received few letters that were manageable to reply in length and objectivity. Nevertheless, the attacks continued.

With the help of our first hired administrator, Mona Jallad, a very capable and a great addition to the Center, I organized our first symposium on Arab-American Economic Relations and discussed it with our Executive Committee. Among its speakers were Gerald Parsky, the Assistant Secretary for International Affairs with the U.S. Department of Treasury, and former Senator J. William Fulbright. I had single-handedly contacted heads of commercial and economic institutions in Washington including Arab embassies to sell them tables of ten at the Center's first major event. I reserved a large hall and even chose the menu for over three hundred in attendance and media representatives at the Shoreham Hotel on Calvert Street. The successful event was held on April 2, 1976, and was well covered by the media.

In the following academic year, Michael Hudson was hired by Georgetown University and became the Center's longest Director. His dedication and clarity of mind pushed the Center to be a world-renowned institution. He organized symposia with in-depth studies not only in Washington but also in the Arab World. With a generous donation from the late Kareema Khoury, he established an annual distinguished lecture. Edward Said (1933-2003) gave the annual distinguished lecture at the Center twice. The seed of his famous work on Orientalism was planted in the first lecture he gave. Other prominent scholars contributed to the intellectually rich library of Kareema Khoury. Before I retired from Georgetown University in 2002, the Center's Director Barbara Stowasser asked me to give a lecture in the same series. It was published under the title, *A View on Islamic Economic Thought.* In addition to Michael C. Hudson there were other notable Directors of the Center for Contemporary Arab Studies: Ibrahim Ibrahim, Hisham Sharaby and Barbara Stowasser.

Based on the CCAS symposia, many books have been published since the nineteen seventies. They have become indispensable scholarly references worldwide. I edited and contributed to two volumes. The first was entitled *The Dynamics of Arab-United States Economic Relations in the 1970s,* published in 1980, with contributions by J. William Fulbright, General George Olmested and Yusif A. Sayigh, myself, and others. The second book was *The Political Economy of Contemporary Egypt,* published in 1990, with contributions by Raymond A. Hinnebusch, Enid Hill, Ibrahim Ibrahim, Charles Issawi Amira Sonbol, myself, and others.

From afar in New Zealand, Peter Krogh, the former dean of the School of Foreign Service who had since retired, wrote me on August 4, 2010, "We have done some great things together including rebuilding the MSFS Program and creating the Center for Contemporary Arab Studies. Along the way, you were an influential, loyal and prized colleague."

I participated in many other scholarly endeavors during these years. The Association of Egyptian-American Scholars was founded by Mohamed El-Wakil, an Egyptian scholar in the field of nuclear engineering. His research and publications in the field had become a worldwide reference. He was one of the first Egyptians to come to the United States right after World War II to pursue their graduate studies. Others came at the same time, including two former prime ministers, Aziz Sedky and Moustafa Khalil, as well as Ashraf Ghorbal, a longtime envoy to the United States who had a distinguished career in serving U.S.-Egyptian relations. In a visit to Egypt in the late nineteen sixties, he had a meeting with Anwar Sadat, then the vice president of the country. He presented to him his vision and that of a small group of distinguished Americans of Egyptian origin to start an Association of Egyptian-American Scholars. The purpose was to create a dialogue between scholars for the benefit of an advancement of research and publications in different disciples of knowledge. Vice President Anwar Sadat gave his full encouragement and support.

The Association of Egyptian-American Scholars (AEAS) was officially registered in the State of Wisconsin by a few pioneers, including me, in the early 1970s. It worked closely with a new organization, Friends of Egyptian Scholars Abroad (FOESA) headed by a former prime minister, Mahmoud Fawzi, a distinguished visionary leader followed by the energetic Mahmoud Mahfouz. After the 1973 October War and the resumption of political relationships between the United States and Egypt, we held our biannual conference under the title "Egypt the Year 2000." We met with President Sadat at Al-Qanatir presidential resort. It was at the water barrage near Cairo constructed in the time of Egypt's ruler Mohamed Ali in the first half of the nineteenth century to regulate the use of the waters of the Nile River.

In the late 1980s, the ambassador of the Sultanate of Oman contacted me to meet with the Minister of Education who was on an official visit to Washington. At that time, he was also the Vice Rector of Sultan Qaboos University. He asked for my advice on establishing a College of Business and Economics at the University. We communicated for about a month after which he asked me to be a founding member of the proposed college. Rawya Saud Al Busaidi, an efficient and highly impressive liaison with a doctorate from Oxford University, arranged for a meeting of all founding members. She held the position of Higher-Education Undersecretary. Later on, she became the first Omani female to be appointed to a ministerial portfolio when she became Oman's Minister of Higher Education effective March 8, 2004, and the president of the Council of Sultan Qaboos University. The Committee of the Founding Members was composed of Michael J. Baker, Professor at Strathclyde University; Ali Elsalmi, Vice Rector of Cairo Univetrsity; Tewfic Gelassi, Professor at Insead; Lord Graham Hills, President of Strathclyde University; Daniel J. Richard, Professor at MIT; and myself. At our first meeting, we elected Ali Elsalmi to chair the committee.

Over the course of two years, we held several meetings under the efficient chairman, who drafted a plan of action and a task for every member until the mission was successfully accomplished. Drawing from the expertise of every one of us in the different fields of accounting, business administration, economics, management, quantitative analysis, we designed a unique curriculum. We also had an input in the architectural design to give students, faculty and researchers a state-of-the-art facility. As a founding member, I am proud that the College of Commerce and Economics at Sultan Qaboos University turned out to be a model to be imitated in other Arab countries and elsewhere.

Throughout my teaching career, I have always been not only a mentor, but also an advisor with open heart and mind to my students. I quibbled, joked and introduced humor every now and then to keep attracting their attention to an otherwise difficult subject. On September 18, 1968, I missed one class where former President

Bill Clinton was a student because of a car accident. After an X-ray at the Georgetown Hospital, my neck was wrapped with an inconvenient support. Two days later, I met my class and before I was asked, "What happened?" I read them the following poem:

> A lady, I thought, could handle her car
> Could step on brakes, could see thus far
> Could stop on red, could start on green
> Could steer the wheel, could park in-between
>
> That lady didn't do ...
> She ran into me.
>
> I was waiting for the green
> Sitting safely in my car
> Here that lady let her car
> jump, in violence, on my car
>
> Interrupting private thoughts!

While students burst into laughter, I noticed honest concern and anxiety that had been expressed by some of them in words, cards, flowers or otherwise kind looks in their innocent eyes.

I shared with my students their personal and national concerns over a cup of Russian tea, a recipe I leared in my early days in Minnesota in 1960, at my apartment or else at coffee shops around campus. Sometimes I cooked light meals for a group of them. When I got married in 1975, I made a habit of inviting the top students over a meal at our home. Some of them became close and remained friends no matter how high their positions may have turned out to be. Tatiana Gfoeller, U.S. ambassador to the Kyrgyz Republic, calls me "uncle Ibrahim." Her husband Michael Gfoeller, also a former student of mine, was promoted to the rank of ambassador in 2010 and Tatiana invited us to their wedding in 1984. They asked my daughter Yasmeen at age 5 to carry flowers behind the bride while my son Kareem at age 4 would carry an icon in a traditional Greek Orthodox wedding. It was an unforgettable wedding at St. Katherine's Church in Falls Church. Our beautiful girl walked down the aisle after the bride holding a big bouquet of flowers. A few steps behind her there was Kareem holding an icon with a serious look on his face, giving the impression of a mature boy who can perfectly accomplish the mission he was entrusted with.

We have been in occasional touch with the Gfoellers ever since. I saw both of them in Saudi Arabia when they served at the U.S. Embassy in Riyadh. While Tatiana speaks Russian fluently since she was raised by her Russian grandmother in Atlanta, Michael learned it before they were assigned to the U.S. Embassy in Moscow. That saved his life. While in Moscow, he and another female diplomat were sent to a mission in Chechnya. As soon as they crossed the border into Chechnya, he heard the conversation between the Russian driver and the other Russian bodyguard assigned to them.

"Why don't we kill these two Americans, take their money, and then say the Chechens killed them?" one asked the other.

"Why kill us?" Michael told them in Russian. "We can give you the money we have. Besides, you may be held accountable for the crime by your superiors if they don't believe your story."

Michael opened his wallet in front of them, pulled out all the money he had and handed it to them. He asked his fellow diplomat to do the same but she was reluctant. Michael was firm, telling her he would explain later. Not knowing the Russian language, she did not know what was going on. Michael informed me that upon reporting the episode, the State Department reimbursed them. It was a practical reminder of the Prophet Muhammad's saying: "Learning the language of another community can protect one against their evils."

Throughout my teaching career I focused on learning and caring for my students no matter how large classes may be. Amidst a class of 150 students, I noticed a girl who was distracted with a painful look on her face. I asked her to see me after class. She informed me that she had lost her mother. I talked with her and took her to our home. Céline and I talked with her about matters related to life and death while having dinner, and introduced our young children to her. I told her that the best she can do to honor the memory of her mother was to take care of her health, do well in her studies and chart carefully her future life in addition to taking care of her younger sisters. I gave her a copy of what I wrote to my children as shown at the beginning of this book. Because of the warm compassion she felt amongst my family, she returned to campus smiling and determined to help herself out. I found out later that she was the niece of Mayor Bill Daley of Chicago.

One time, while going through the student classroom roster, I spotted a familiar name. I called on the student.

"Your last name is familiar to me. In the past, did I teach a brother or a sister of yours?" I asked.

"No, sir," the student replied. "You taught my father."

I found out that there were two similar cases in the same class. I thought of inviting the three students and their parents at home over couscous deliciously cooked by our Moroccan live-in house-keeper. It was not a coincidence that they ended up in my class. Once admitted to Georgetown University, their parents advised them to take my course.

Since results of tests may not completely reflect students true grasp of the material being taught, I never relied on only one examination. Instead, I give three quizzes throughout the course, weekly assignments and a term paper. If a student shows to improve during the course, his or her grade would reflect it by giving less weight to the quiz in which the performance was less than the others. My philosophy of teaching is based on learning and education rather than penalization, on recognition of improvement and encouragement rather than dependency on simple mathematical additions of scores, a scale allowing for recognition for better performance and class participation. By the same token, I never use the same notes year after year, since there are always new advances in the field and new developments in the world.

While it is important in one's life to have good education, to earn a living and to raise family, I believe it is a duty for every person to serve his/her community and society. I applied such philosophy to my self. In addition to government affiliations and military service, I have always been involved with civic and non-governmental organizations, be it in Egypt as shown above or in the United States as noted below.

Council on Egyptian-American Relations

In early 1998, I invited a small group of distinguished career diplomats to lunch at the garden terrace of the Four Seasons Hotel in Georgetown. They included: Le Roy Alfred Atherton, U.S. ambassador to Egypt (1979–83), Lucius Derham Battle, U.S. ambassador to Egypt (1964–67), Andrew I. Killgore, U.S. ambassador to Egypt and Qatar (1976–80) and the publisher of the widely circulated *Washington Report on Middle East Affairs*, Robert H. Pelletreau, U.S. ambassador to Egypt (1991–93), and Edward W. Walker, U.S. ambassador to Egypt (1994–97). I presented the idea of establishing a Council on Egyptian-American Relations. They blessed such efforts and agreed to serve on its board along with others. Ambassador Killgore commented, "Such an institution is long overdue."

I rushed to have its bylaws completed and have it legally formed. I chose an office not far from my office at Georgetown University so that I would not waste time commuting. Thanks to a prominent lawyer and close friend of mine, William Joyce, CEAR was granted tax-exempt status. Hence, it was established as a non-profit educational institution in 1999 to help promote a strong relationship between Egypt and the United States for their strategic and economic interests. We thought the occasion of a U.S.-Egyptian summit meeting in Washington, D.C. in March 2000, would be an opportunity to launch CEAR's inaugural event. We held several conferences both in Washington and in Cairo. I was invited to the U.S. Department of State for briefings and consultations. Television and other networks both in the United States and Egypt often contacted me to comment on recent developments. I was invited to the White House when there were summit meetings between President Clinton and President Hosni Mubarak.

Faith and Hope

Shortly after the October 1973 war in which Egypt was able militarily and politically to regain Sinai from an Israeli occupation, Mrs. Jehan Sadat, the wife of Anwar Sadat, formed a non-profit organization called Faith and Hope to help the injured from war casualties. I established a chapter in the United States with the purpose of raising funds for her project. In her official visit to Washington accompanying her husband the late President Sadat, I asked her to cut the ribbon at the newly established office of Faith and Hope in the United States.

The Jones Institute

In the early 1980s, Howard Jones informed me that he planned to retire from the Johns Hopkins University Medical School, and that Eastern Virginia Medical School through his old colleague Mason Andrews asked him to establish the Jones Institute in Norfolk Virginia.

"Can you help me?" he asked.

"Of course, Howard, I am indebted to you," I said. "You resolved the fertility problem that my wife had without a mess of an operation. Thanks to you, we have two children."

At the first meeting convened at Eastern Virginia Medical School, we discussed the future plans of the Jones Institute for Reproductive Medicine. I was nominated to be the first Chairman of the Board. I served in that capacity for nearly a decade until the breaking of the grounds of the Jones Institute in 1990

Pioneering research in the Jones Institute resulted in the publication of pioneering articles on the high incidence and significance of male factor infertility and the realization that IVF could overcome most of these problems. IVF was therefore understood as a technology that could successfully treat all female and male infertility problems. It was at the Jones Institute in 1989 that the first attempts to overcome the most severe sperm anomalies using microinjection techniques took place, but although fertilization of the eggs occurred, no pregnancies were established. In 1992, the first birth from this technique called ICSI (intracytoplasmic sperm injection) occurred and ICSI is now state-of-the-art for treating male infertility. In the early 1990s, the first pregnancies following preimplantation genetic diagnosis (PGD) from biopsied embryos were reported in Europe. The Jones Institute reported the first live birth in the world after PGD for the potentially lethal Tay-Sachs disease in 1996. These techniques are now routinely offered to couples that are carriers of certain chromosomal and genetic defects.

Since the mid-1980s, IVF has been augmented by the possibility to freeze supernumerary embryos. Since then, more that 12,000 embryos have been frozen at Norfolk, and upon thawing and transfering have helped hundreds of couples to conceive. The Jones Institute is responsible for the birth of almost 4,000 babies treated in Norfolk. A large number of clinicians and scientists from IVF centers in the United States and the rest of the world from all continents have been trained in Norfolk, and the Jones Institute has therefore gained an international reputation as an academic center. In 2010, the Jones Institute reported on a live birth that followed the transfer of embryos that were frozen for almost 20 years! This is the first of such reports, which also confirms the success as well as safety of this technique. The Jones Institute has also pioneered discussions and establishment of guidelines governing ART at the level of the American Society for Reproductive Medicine. As such, the growth of IVF and other ART has always followed the highest ethical standards and accreditation from the newly established regulatory agencies.

In a celebration of his upcoming 100th birthday on September 21, 2010, the President of the Eastern Virginia Medical School, Harry Lester, welcomed over 200 guests and introduced me as the first Chairman of the Foundation of the Jones Institute in the early 1980s. I concluded my brief talk by saying: "Dr. Howard Jones is a rare phenomenon with super energy of mind. He is an icon of accomplishments who continues his mission in life with the same ingenuity known about him." I was followed by the current chairman, Howard Milstein, whose generosity and commitment had enabled the fundraising efforts under my tenure to pay for the cost of the construction of the Jones Institute at Eastern Virginia Medical School.

Arab-American University Graduates

In the late 1960s, a group of us including Ibrahim Abu Lughod, Hassan Haddad, Hisham Sharaby, Edward Said, Clovis Maksoud, Elaine Hagopian, Cherif Bassiouni, Afaf Mahfouz, Bahaa Abou Laban, and me among other notable Arab-American scholars became active in the newly formed AAUG, Arab-American University Graduates. We held an annual conference in different locations in the United States. Once, we were invited to have our conference in Kuwait by the energetic Salem Al Sabah, who was his country's ambassador to the United States.

I was elected for one term as the national vice president and the president of its chapter in Washington, D.C. We presented in-depth studies and published a periodical advocating fairness and justice for the Palestinians and for all those suffering from discrimination and who were robbed of their inalienable rights of self-determination. I formed a committee in 1972 to raise funds with the purpose of renting an office for "Palestine House" at Dupont Circle in Washington. It was a forum for education, debate and understanding the complexities of the Arab-Israeli conflict. I was elected its president, but my right arm was Anis Kassim, a Palestinian studying law with a prominent authority in international law at George Washington Law Center, Tom Mallison. Among its speakers were highly prominent personalities such as Fayez Sayegh, Tahseen Basheer, Edward Said and Clovis Maksoud.

When I turned seventy on September 25, 2001, I thought it was time for me to retire. As indicated earlier, I wrote to the President of the University, Leo J. O'Donovan: "Dear Leo, Professors go through five stages in their lives: tireless, tiring, tiresome, tired, and then retired. Even though I am still tireless, yet it is time for me to retire." He liked the note, and indeed followed suit soon after.

Upon my retirement, I received an overwhelming number of letters from my former students, the President of the United States George W. Bush, the King of Jordan Abdullah, the President of Georgetown University John J. DeGioia, and Jane Dammen McAuliffe, the dean of the Georgetown College. Robert L. Gallucci, the dean of Georgetown University Edmund A. Walsh School of Foreign Service, held an elaborate dinner for the occasion at the Georgetown Club in which he awarded me the Dean's Medal, a precious crystal pyramid, often given to heads of states and high dignitaries.

The respect and affection that the students had for me were overwhelming and gratifying. I was honored that Carroll Round initiated an annual lecture under my name. Carroll Round is an annual international economic conference at Georgetown University School of Foreign Service. It was instituted in 2002 to provide a unique forum for research and discussion among the undergraduates from the United States leading universities. The highly reputable Carroll Round was initiated and managed by a group of my best students, Chris Griffin, Andrew Hayashi, Scott Pedovitz, Robert Katz, Kika Pluta, Meredith Gilbert, and Erica Yu. Chris and his committee were able to raise the necessary funds through a generous donation from Sallie May Fund and other contributors.

Dr. Larry Lindsay, Chairman of the President's Council of Economic Advisors, gave the first Ibrahim M. Oweiss lecture on April 6, 2002, at the Georgetown University Riggs Library. Speakers in the following years included Dr. Hubbard in 2003 addressing the topic of An Agenda for Global Growth; in 2004 by Peter R. Orszag, Senior Fellow at the Brookings Institution and later President Obama's budget director; in 2005 by Dr. William Easterly, Professor at New York University; in 2006 by Dr. Kemal Dervis, the head of the United Nations Development Programme (UNDP); and in 2007 by Dr. François Bourguignon, the Chief Economist and Senior Vice President at the World Bank.

I thought I had bidden farewell to teaching and to Georgetown. A year after I retired, I was honored to be nominated and elected to serve as a Regent in continuation of my service to the institution I joined in 1967. In my new capacity, I was involved in our collective recommendations and a plan for fund raising to cope with the ever-increasing demand for financial resources to fund our expanding facilities, research and increase in enrollment. We held two major events annually in which the president of the University as well as the Provost and deans gave their reports followed by discussions and recommendations.

During that time, I was informed of an on-going negotiation to establish a branch of Georgetown University's School of Foreign Service in Qatar. I was on my way to the Healy building after I had just returned from a trip to Kuwait and Qatar in early May 2005. I ran into Robert Gallucci, the Dean of the School of Foreign Service (SFS), and James Reardon-Anderson, the Chair of the SFS faculty.

"Do you want to go to Qatar?" Jim said.

"Yes," I replied.

With a handshake, we went our separate ways. Jim afterwards informed me that SFS had just reached an agreement with Qatar Foundation to open its branch in Qatar in August 2005. Upon outlining his offer to me, I accepted to return to teaching, this time

7000 miles from the main campus. Jim was appointed the dean of the School Foreign Service in Qatar, which had become known as SFS-Q. And so I returned to teaching from 2005 until the first class we admitted in that year graduated in May 2009, after which I retired for the second time.

On my way to Qatar in August 2005, I flew first from Washington to Morocco to attend its 27th annual International Cultural *Moussem* and symposium under the patronage of His Majesty King Mohammed VI in Assilah. It was held at the Hassan II Center for International Conventions. The symposium theme was, "Arabs and Americans: The Images of One in the Eyes of the Other." It was as usual culturally stimulating. Among the participants were good friends such as the late Ahmed Maher, the former Egyptian Minister of Foreign Affairs and former ambassador to the United States. He spoke eloquently about American double standards, treating Israel with utmost support of its policies, right or wrong, while treating all others with another yardstick. Israel used the one-word vocabulary of the Bush administration, namely terrorism, to label all resistance of occupation as acts of terrorism and hence deny the Palestinians their inalienable right of self-determination.

The paper I presented was based on a poll I conducted throughout the months of June and July 2005. A simple random sample of 1000 inhabitants of the Pinellas County, in the western parts of Florida, was conducted. It was this specific county that had tipped the extremely close 2000 presidential election in favor of George W. Bush by narrowly winning the electorate vote over Al Gore who won the popular vote. The simple random sample was composed of 48 percent males and 52 percent females, 97 percent finished high school education and 41 percent had college degrees.

Results of the poll were as follows:

For general knowledge about Arab countries, their locations and their elementary history: Only 11 percent came up with correct answers, while 89 percent were in the dark concerning basic knowledge of the Arab countries.

What is the religion of the Arabs? 76 percent said Islam.

Are there Christian Arabs? 92 percent said no.

Are there Muslims other than Arabs? 71 percent said no.

Is Egypt an Arab country? 67 percent said no.

What is it then? 59 percent said Pharaonic.

Do you agree now with the decision of the United States to go to war against Iraq? 82 percent said NO.

Did you agree, then at the time when the war began, with the decision of the United States to go to war against Iraq? 49 percent said NO.

What is the core cause of the Arab-Israeli conflict? 57 percent said "terrorism against Israel", 41 percent said "Arabs do not have peace with Israel"

Is there a peace between Egypt and Israel? 63 percent said NO.

Is there a peace between Jordan and Israel? 51 percent said NO.

Do you have the same perception of the Arabs after September 11, 2001? 24 percent said NO.

Worse? 59 percent said YES.

At the symposium, I was impressed by the perceptive remarks and interventions not only from top thinkers from the Arab countries, Africa, Europe, the United States, and elsewhere, but also by the youth from Assilah expressing themselves mostly in the Arabic or in the French languages. Whichever they chose, their views were understood by all participants, thanks to the modern and efficient simultaneous interpretation that Mohamed Benaissa had effectively instituted.

I had known Benaissa since my days in Minnesota, and we have never lost touch with one another. I was a groomsman at his wedding. Upon graduation from the University of Minnesota's journalism school, he joined the Moroccan delegation at the United Nations in New York to assume the position of the Information Officer at the United Nations Headquarters before being assigned to the UN Commission for Africa (ECA) stationed in Ethiopia. He had another move when he was appointed the Regional Information Advisor for Africa for the UN Food and Agricultural Organization (FAO) stationed in Accra, Ghana. Benaissa spent seven years working for the UN system in Africa before moving to FAO's headquarters in Rome, where he was appointed the Director of Information

Division. We corresponded with one another and we met whenever he came for vacations in the United States. As he settled afterwards in Italy's beautiful capital at FAO's headquarters, I used to make a point of stopping in Rome on my way to the Middle East even for one day just to have a visit with my dear friend until he resigned and returned to Assilah, his birthplace town in Morocco. It was in Rome that he and his first wife Carole got separated leading later to a divorce. By that time he had two daughters, Shafiah and Nihal.

Back in Assilah, he ran for the city and parliamentary elections and won. He thought for years to find the best modality for the development of his birthplace. His years of experience in Africa and later as the Director of Information Division with the United Nations Food and Agricultural Organization in Rome (FAO), and earlier in Ethiopia, had convinced him that the road to development runs through self reliance and people's participation. He thought of culture as a means to arouse the community interest, and communication as a way to call the attention of public and private sectors to the economic potentials of his hometown. He was also concerned with making out of Assilah an international platform for dialogue between cultures and civilizations. In 1977, he wrote his thoughts on his way to visit me when I was ambassador in New York. I was the first one to be exposed to his innovative ideas and plans for Assilah. I became enthusiastic about the creation of cultural events to which artists, painters, musicians and others can congregate during a special month. The modality of Cannes in France was on his mind with modifications to suit Morocco, Africa and the Arab world. The first cultural festival, called *Moussem*, was held in July 1978 and has been successfully planned and implemented—and growing—ever since.

He was remarried to a superbly beautiful lady from Morocco, Laila Hajoui, whose father was an eminent scholar. She had a Masters degree in Library Science from the University of Maryland in the United States. Laila's gentle and quiet demeanor was a perfect complement to Mohamed's dynamism. He was appointed the Minister of Culture from 1985 to 1992. Among other accomplishments in that post, to his credit, Mohamed Benaissa assembled the remaining musicians in Morocco still playing Andalusia Music. With limited budget of his ministry, he was able to raise the necessary funds to produce and preserve the biggest anthology of Andalusia music in 72 CDs. My wife and I were elated when he was appointed the Moroccan ambassador to the United States in 1993 at the beginning of the first term of President Bill Clinton in the White House.

He opened many doors through diplomacy and cultural exchange. He seized the opportunity that Chelsea Clinton was attending the Sidwell Friends, a Quaker private school in Washington, to bring a group of musicians from Fas to play the traditional Andalusia music, which President and Mrs. Clinton attended. He brought the works of famous painters to be prominently displayed in the capital of the United States. When the late King Hassan came to Washington, President Clinton called Mohamed Benaissa his friend and congratulated the King for his superb choice of the ambassador.

Because of his electrifying success in Washington, the King summoned him in 1999 to Morocco and appointed him the Minister of Foreign Affairs and Cooperation. Mohamed Benaissa served highly successfully in that post for nearly nine years after Minister Abdellatif Filali, and thus became the longest minister of Foreign Affairs in Morocco since its independence in 1956. Following his love for the arts and history, he ordered the publication of an outstanding book, *Art and Diplomacy*, in which rare collections of pictures and paintings to be found only in national archives were reproduced, and a thousand years of diplomatic history of Morocco was briefly documented.

Whether as a Mayor of Assilah, a member of the Parliament, Minister of Culture, ambassador to Washington or Minister of Foreign Affairs and Cooperation, he is always organizing superb Assilah *Moussems* with an international conference discussing topical themes in which thinkers, diplomats, policy makers, academicians, writers, journalists and representatives from the media, non-governmental organizations, United Nations, UNESCO and others congregate each August. It was in Assilah that the theme of globalization was first discussed as soon as the topic became known in the early 1990's. I am proud to have been attending and contributing to those conferences for the last three decades.

Thanks to Benaissa's hard work and vision, it was through the arts and culture that Assilah, the small town in which its inhabitants lived within the walls of a fortress overlooking the Atlantic

Ocean, flourished and expanded beyond its original walls. Benaissa was able to build a permanent location, Hassan II Cultural Center for International Conventions, in which an air-conditioned auditorium with a simultaneous translation facility was built, along with three large halls and a gallery for art exhibits in the midst of a rectangular area where plants and greenery are placed in corners and along the sides. Tables and chairs are scattered for participants to enjoy sipping Moroccan tea or coffee while engaging in serious or social conversations. In the artistically designed auditorium there is a large well-equipped stage on which opening ceremonies take place or otherwise musical performances or plays are held. As one enters the fortress through a narrow opening in its six-foot thick wall, the Center stands forty feet away on the right facing the Great Mosque across a narrow road no more than fifteen feet wide. There are a few other much narrower streets of no more than five feet, with white and blue low buildings. Melehi and Farid Belkahia, another renowned artist, designed street pavements in the shape of waves in concrete. Superb, colorful frescos painted on the walls of old Medina adjacent to a school, attract one's eyes while walking towards a road parallel to the sea shore beneath the thick walls of the fortress.

Benaissa instilled in Assilah's residents pride in their town. I saw a young boy rushing to pick up a candy wrap thrown in the street and put it in a trash can. Those are installed everywhere following regulations that Benaissa initiated when he served in his town's municipality. He managed to have an old Portuguese castle restored, with a state-of-the-art library donated by Prince Bandar bin Sultan, the former Saudi Arabia's ambassador to the United States.

In the early years of the *Moussem*, the late King Hassan summoned Mohamed Benaissa to meet with him. The King, known for his astute observation and deep thinking, asked him "What do you plan to do with the Assilah Forum?" It was a golden opportunity for Mohamed Benaissa to explain in concise form his program, but adding that many intellectuals he wishes to invite to speak are left out of the center. The King replied, "You have my endorsement. Make out of Assilah another Hyde Park corner."

The King met with the highly respectable African statesman,

the former President Léopold Senghor, who was invited to speak at the Assilah conference. The then-Crown Prince, who later upon the death of his father ascended to the throne of Morocco, came several times to Assilah including the opening of Prince Bandar bin Sultan Library. In fact, King Mohamed VI has been the Honorary Chairman ever since the inception of Assilah Cultural *Moussem* when he was the Crown Prince.

Discussions continued outside the auditorium in the hallways or at tables scattered at the rectangular center while sipping Moroccan mint tea, coffee, or soft drinks. Masterpieces of artwork by Malika Agueznay, Mohamed Melehi, Ahmad Amrani, Saad Chaffaj, Meki Megara, Joseph Niebla, Martin Prado, Domaso Ruano, Younes El-Kharraz, Saad Tazi, Dima Rachid and others were on the walls. Viewers carry along with them a colorfully decorated catalogue with a brief background of each artist and the name of every exhibited painting. Even the outside walls of the Portuguese fortress are covered with enormous paintings that keep changing from one *Moussem* to another.

A big hit of the Assilah *Moussem* was the participation of famous Arab movie stars drawing crowds around them at the Hassan II Cultural Center for International Conventions, at Prince Bandar Library, or else in the streets or the Old Medina, with its restaurants extended along a wide avenue well lit and blocked off from traffic with thousands of pedestrians walking enjoying the ocean to the west and people-watching in coffee shops to the east.

Before my flight to Qatar, I had the pleasure once again to distribute the financial prizes I donate to the top students from Assilah with the highest scores earned at the end of their high school education. I thought of initiating such a tradition to encourage excellence amongst the youth of Assilah.

On my way to Qatar from Casablanca, I reminisced about my experience with the country, of which I had become fond over the years. In fact, I got to know the country even before I set foot in it. Following its termination of a special treaty on September 3, 1971, with the United Kingdom ending a long-term relationship as its protectorate, the Amiri Diwan asked the World Bank to provide technical assistance to establish its monetary system and its central bank. Abdel-Gelil El-Emary, the Vice President of the International Bank of Reconstruction and Development, abbreviated later on as the World Bank, contacted me to provide him with a study leading to the establishment of Qatar's monetary system and its central bank. We worked on its implementation for ten months. In the course of its creation, Abdel-Gelil Emary asked me to be his Deputy Governor of Qatar's Central Bank, but I had to turn the offer down for professional reasons. My first visit to Qatar was in 1975, when its Minister of Petroleum, Sheikh Abdel-Aziz Ben Khalifa Al-Thani, asked for economic advice before an OPEC meeting. I met the Emir Sheikh Khalifa Bin Hamad Al-Thani and his Chief of Protocol Dr. Issa Ghanem Al-Kawari, who had immensely impressed me by his knowledge, his organizational skills, and his superb analytical abilities.

On my way to Qatar in 1976 for a meeting with the Minister of Petroleum, I sat next to the Egyptian architect Kamal El-Kafrawi from Paris to Doha. He had been living and working in France. He informed me that in 1973, with UNESCO's participation, a preliminary study was launched aiming at the creation of higher education facilities in the State of Qatar. He was awarded the responsibility for the overall design and planning of Qatar University. The gifted architect told me he had to study the design of old buildings in Qatar before the discovery of oil. He found out that a back high wall was to be erected in such a way as to allow a circular flow of air in the premises. He invited me to see the prototype at the place allocated for him and his aides. As a result, the first phase of the project comprising the academic buildings was inaugurated in February 1985.

I gave two public lectures at the newly established university. The first was on the "Pricing of Oil in World Trade and Economics of Petrodollars" and the second was on "Ibn Khaldun, the Father of Economics" in its hall named afterwards as Ibn Khaldun Hall. I have been providing the Amiri Diwan ever since with periodical economic reports including two major studies, one in which I revealed that the United States had charged a premium on its military sales to Iran and to the Arab countries, yet without including the most sophisticated parts, which it only gave Israel to ensure the latter's continued military superiority in the Middle East. The second major study was on "Energy in China," in which I predicted, given its continuous economic growth, that it would enter the oil international market as a buyer after becoming self-sufficient, and that would have an impact on its price.

I flew to Qatar in the third week of August 2005, this time to reside for four years. Thanks to efficient communication with Junie Nathani, the head of the human resources at Georgetown University in Doha, I knew exactly where to head directly from the airport to my living quarters. It was a brand new compound with 48 villas, each of which had three apartments. The apartment allocated to me was a fully furnished three-bedroom apartment on the ground floor. Next to my door, there was another door leading to a staircase for the two units above me. There was a majestic entrance with 24-hour guards, a superb clubhouse with swimming pool, whirlpool, sauna, restaurant, pool table, computer room with access to the Internet and an office to manage the whole complex.

Qatar has become dedicated to progress under its current rulers. The ruler of Qatar, Sheikh Hamad bin Khalifa Al Thani, and his wife, Sheikha Mozah bint Nasser, are considered by neutral observers to be the most progressive Muslim leaders. Sheikh Hamad bin Khalifa has taken power in 1995 in a bloodless coup. Ever since his first years in office, Sheikh Hamad has set the country on a path of modernization and progress while still keeping and preserving the country's traditions and culture. Their vision of a modern state of Qatar has focused on developing modern state institutions, a state-of-the-art educational system and a modern healthcare system. In addition, they directed their energies and the resources of the state of Qatar on promoting peace and peaceful co-existence regionally and internationally.

Education, which is the basis of all facets of development, has undergone major reforms in Qatar under the direction of Sheikha Mozah. The reforms have included all educational institutions from pre-school to higher education. All government-sponsored schools are being transformed into independent schools that are governed by independent school councils under the direction of the higher supreme education council, which she chairs. The independent schools placed a greater emphasis on essential life skills such as critical thinking, research and teamwork. Qatar Education City is now home to six campuses of prestigious universities, including Carnegie Mellon University, Georgetown University, Texas A&M University, Virginia Commonwealth University, Northwestern University, and Weill Cornell Medical School. In addition, it includes a Qatar Science and Technology Park, and various research centers, including Sidra Medical and Research Center and the Social Development Center. The Emir and Sheikha Mozah are also recognized regionally and internationally for the establishment of the Shafallah Center for Children with Special Needs. The Center ensures that children with special needs will receive the most effective instruction and training.

The Emir of Qatar has chosen a path of political pragmatism from the early days of his reign. He led successful peace talks for Lebanon, Sudan, Yemen, and the Palestinian authority. The Emir has also utilized the vast resources of Qatar in natural gas to build and modernize his country and to help fellow Arab and Muslim countries. In addition, he has contributed generously to the rebuilding of countries that suffered major natural disasters, including Katrina in United States and the Tsunami in Indonesia. The state of Qatar under his rule has become a model country in building state-of-the-art infrastructure and in improving the lives of its citizens.

Knowing that culture and sports are vehicles and platforms for successful peaceful co-existence and diplomacy, the Emir and his wife have invested heavily in both areas. These efforts have resulted in the establishments of museums and art galleries, including the well known Islamic Museum and Museum for Modern Arabic Art. In addition, Qatar has hosted the Asian Games 2006 and the Asian Cup 2011. Those efforts have culminated in the choice of Qatar to host the World Cup in 2022.

The Emir and his wife Sheikha Mozah have promoted the critical and essential role of modern media and communications in supporting change and development. Qatar is the home for the most-watched TV channel in the Middle East, Al Jazeera. In addition, the Emir and his wife Sheikha Mozah promoted freedom of speech, freedom of the press, and human rights both locally and across the globe.

I have been an eyewitness observing how Qatar has wisely been using its natural resources by investing in high-quality education as well as in its construction sector and its overall development. Furthermore, it has been rising to prominence in Arab culture and has become a world center for discussion of global issues. It has also been laboriously involved in settling regional disputes, be it in Lebanon, in Sudan, among the Palestinian factions, in the Middle East peace process, or elsewhere.

Qatar is a small country with enormous natural resources making itself big through its wise leadership ever since it came to power in 1995, its dedication to high quality education and its ability to capture the modern essence of knowledge economy, creative society and information technology. My former student Dr. Xiaoxing Han, currently residing and working in Hong Kong, elaborated that it was fitting to call it a "collaborative economy." The Qatari leadership comprehends the value of partnership with the best in several domains from the furthest corners of the world.

I firmly believe that the Emir Sheikh Hamad Al-Thani and Sheikha Mozah Al-Misned deserve the Nobel Peace Prize for what they have been contributing to the field of education and to world affairs, and for their prominence in settling national and regional disputes. This made their capital one of the important global pivots for the well-known Doha Round for free trade, referred to in any textbook on international economics taught at universities around the world.

On the morning after my arrival, we all mounted a minibus to Education City, an immense integrated educational project on a 2500-acre flat area in the midst of a desert on the outskirts of Doha. Georgetown University had some temporary offices in a section of the high school. After being greeted by our dean James Reardon-Anderson, we were ushered to the office of Allyson Handley, who gave each of us a cellular phone and provided us with basic information on the orientation program.

With enthusiasm to pursue my beloved teaching profession, I met my classes with the same dynamism as I had always had in the past in spite of my age. An esteemed colleague of mine, Gary Wasserman, called me "an energizer."

Georgetown University School of Foreign Service in Qatar (SFS-Q) was temporarily located in an ingeniously structured white building called LAS (Liberal Arts & Science) with numerous openings scattered at different angles and shapes through which, when it gets dark, light shines like scattered diamonds from afar. The Academic Bridge Program, preparing students for college education in the English language and teaching other subjects including computer training, was housed in the same building, as well as Texas A & M University until its building was completed in 2007, and Carnegie Mellon University until the construction of its spacious campus was finished in 2008.

Georgetown University School of Foreign Service was not the first to establish a campus in the vast area of Qatar Foundation for Education, Science and Community Development, which was created upon an issuance of an Amiri Decree in 1995, nor was it the last. It was during a visit to Qatar in 1996 to give the Distinguished Public Lecture on the economics of oil, that Khalid Al Manei, the son of a good friend of mine, Abdulla Al-Manei, the first Qatari ambassador to the United States whom I had known since he was born, came to me after the lecture to greet me and to invite me to the then modest office of Qatar Foundation.

Sheikha Mozah built a world-renowned empire of education in Qatar. She brought in the best possible team to help the development and growth of institutions that would have remarkable impact not only in Qatar but also in the entire Middle East. The city of Qatar Foundation with its more than 2,500 students covers three quarters the area of Cambridge, Massachusetts, that includes two of the top Universities in the world: Harvard University and Massachusetts Institute of Technology.

Of course, it is not a matter of size that can bring a lasting impact on a nation or a region. High quality education was the main goal of Qatar Foundation under the chairmanship of its founder Sheikha Mozah. She has been able to attract six well-known universities from the United States, and possibly others in the future. In order of inauguration in Qatar, they were as follows: Virginia Commonwealth University, Weill Cornell Medical College, Texas A & M University, Carnegie Mellon University, Georgetown University School of Foreign Service, and Northwestern University. In addition, Qatar Faculty of Islamic Studies was established in 2007. Sheikha Mozah had been looking for the best talents in the field of education to be the pillars of Qatar Foundation. She chose a prominent figure, Charles E. Young, the Chancellor Emeritus and Professor of Political Science, Public Policy, and Management of the University of California Los Angeles (UCLA) School of Public Affairs and an internationally recognized leader of higher education, to serve as the President of Qatar Foundation from 2004 to 2006.

An outstanding successor Dr. Mohamed Fathy Saoud who was with the original creating team of Qatar Foundation (QF) since 1997, first as Higher Education to its Board of Directors then as a member of the Board in 2003, was named by Sheikha Mozah to assume the position of QF's President in November 2007 and the Vice-Chairman of the Board of Governors and Chairman of the Executive Committee of the Foundation's Sidra Medical and Research Center. A scientist who earned his Ph.D. degree in the United Kingdom at an early age of 25, he started his academic career climbing the ladder quickly. He came to Qatar from Egypt in the early 1970s to help Dr. Mahmoud Kazem, originally from Aswan Egypt, to transform his college of education in Qatar into a full-fledged university. Dr. Saoud became the youngest dean of the faculty of science in the Arab countries when he founded it at Qatar University and remained in that position for ten years. He has been instrumental in the planning and development of Education City, Qatar Foundation's flagship project, and had undoubtedly played an important role in the visionary planning of many projects in Education City including the university campuses, Sidra Medical School and Research Center, and Qatar National Research Fund. In my encounter with him, I found him to be a man of vision, a doer of the first order, a quiet thinker and a systematic planner. In addition to Dr. Saoud, Sheikha Mozah gathered a high-powered team including Nobel Laureate Dr. Ahmed Zewail, Dr. Saif Al-Hajari as Vice Chairman, the President of Qatar University Dr. Sheikha Al-Misned, Dr. Jordan J. Cohen, renowned in the field of medicine, Dr. Vartan Gregorian, the president of Carnegie Corporation, Qatar's Minister of Finance Dr. Yousef Hussain Kamal, and Dr. Ahmed Zaki Yamani, former Saudi Minister of Petroleum and Mineral Resources.

Qatar Academy was the first institution of Education City in 1996 to provide high quality learning for children from kindergarten to high school. Fourteen years later, it opened a branch in north Qatar. Qatar Leadership Academy, a boarding military school for boys, was also established in Qatar Foundation. Students with learning deficiencies find a welcoming school in the Learning School with a highly specialized director and instructors in the fields of child psychology and training. It was thought that a Music Academy could be a forthcoming project for Education City. Qatar Foundation is indeed reshaping the country and its economy around three core pillars: education, science through research, and community development.

In addition to meetings my students in small classes, I was frequently interviewed in the national and international media. I lectured widely and participated in tens of conferences.

Despite its small size, I found Qatar to be culturally rich. In the first semester in Qatar in 2005, I gave a public lecture on globalization and its consequences in both rich and poor nations. I argued convincingly that in spite of some of its negative results such as outsourcing and its effect on unemployment in the United States and the undesirable consequences of its spread in developing nations, the positive aspects of globalization outweigh others for the economic benefit of the world community. As an educator, I felt all along that it was my duty not only to keep digging for the truth but also to convey my findings beyond classroom walls.

In the meanwhile, as I had always done, I brought the world I knew to my students. For example, I managed to get Lord Browne of Madingley, the Group Executive Director of British Petroleum, to converse with my students in Qatar in 2006 while he was touring the countries of the Middle East. Having had Mohamed, a son of the Emir of Qatar, in my class, I was pleasantly surprised to have received a call from the Amiri Diwan to inform me that the Amir accompanying his visitor Sheikh Mohamed Bin Rashid, the ruler of Dubai, was on his way to visit Georgetown University in 2006. I hurried downstairs to the Dean's office. Jim Reardon-Anderson and I stood at the entrance of the LAS Building. The Emir embraced me and introduced his prominent guest whom I met for the first time even though I had met his father when I addressed a world conference on oil in 1976. The two dignitaries sat down in the Hoya student lounge between the Dean and me. It was a moment of great honor to have students in proximity conversing with two heads of state.

Less than a month after the visit, I felt a pain in my chest. I went first to the American Hospital in Doha, but I was advised to go to Doha Hospital Clinic, an extremely clean and well-organized hospital that referred me to the immense Doha Hospital to use the ultra sophisticated medical equipment.

After thorough tests, Abdel-Aziz Al-Khulaifi, a well-known heart surgeon turned to me and said, "You have a blockage in what we call the `widow artery' because a blockage in it will make your wife a widow. You need a quadruple bypass."

"Is it that serious?" I asked. "Do I have time to have the operation done in the United States?"

"I am afraid not," the doctor replied.

I agreed to have the surgery performed on September 25, 2006, the day of my 75th birthday. I said that to him as if I were talking about a minor scratch on my hand. I am a firm believer in God's will. Whatever is meant to be will take place with or without our actions and deeds. On my way to campus, I chatted with my driver Hamed as if nothing had happened. Hamed had a degree from Al-Azhar University in Islamic Studies and was an Imam leading prayers and giving sermons on Fridays and other religious holidays. He had a superb voice in reciting the Holy Q'uran.

I went straight to meet the dean, James Reardon-Anderson. After having explained the matter so that he would make the necessary arrangements for Ganesh Seshan, the only other economist at SFS-Q, to teach my class, I told him, "There is no way my wife could be with me in less than 20 hours from now. Please do not inform my family in the United States." He honored my request.

At 6:00 a.m., Hamed came to pick me up from my residency at Samyria Gardens and we went directly to the hospital. I was placed on a bed to have anesthesia performed on me and kept talking to the physician until I was gone. I did not feel a thing neither did I see the theater where surgeries take place. My bed was wheeled from one place to another until I found myself in a private room on the sixth floor. When I woke up, I saw a bearded surgeon next to me.

"I am Dr. Rashid Mazhar. I assisted Dr. Abdel-Aziz Al-Khulaifi," he introduced himself."

"How did it go?" I asked.

"It was successfully performed," he assured me.

I called Céline. "I have good news and bad news," I began.

"What happened?" she asked.

"The bad news is that I had a blockage in four arteries needing a quadruple bypass. The good news is that the heart surgery was performed yesterday. I was just told that the operation was successful," I said.

A few minutes later, my daughter Yasmeen called to tell me how angry she was for me not informing the family. She was talking and crying over the phone. I meant to put her at ease across the 7,000 miles separating us. I was worried that her emotions might affect her in her seventh month of her pregnancy. She handed the phone to her husband Mark. I talked to Kareem and Julie in Rwanda. The very efficient head of our human resources at Georgetown University in Qatar, Junie Nathani, a distinguished lady from a prominent Indian family, arranged for my wife to come from Washington.

On my third day after the surgery, I asked if I could walk slowly to the front desk of my ward to check my email. It was an utter surprise for our Dean Jim Reardon Anderson and Junie Nathani when they were on their way to visit me in my room. Even with his cool Anglo-Saxon restraint, he could not help it raising both hands up with disbelief, while Junie had her usual kind smile, and a surprised look.

In the meanwhile, some 7,000 miles away, the chair of the French Department, Debbie Lesko Baker, made a quick replacement for Céline's classes while the faculty conveyed their heartfelt sentiments to her.

In Qatar, Hussein Al-Dobashi, a human resources officer at Georgetown University School of Foreign Service, had gone completely out of his way to make sure that Céline would be comfortable upon arrival and throughout her stay with me on a couch adjacent to my bed for one whole month. An infection was spotted that necessitated another anesthesia and a second operation in my chest while Céline was with me holding my hand until the bed I was lying on was wheeled to the operating room once again. Every working day, a group of doctors would surround my bed examining and asking questions while nurses would do their daily routine work of blood analysis, electrocardiogram charts, and giving me the medications I needed including insulin for diabetes. Dr. Rashid Mazhar had gone beyond the call of duty, visiting me on weekends and holidays, even at a time when his wife delivered a baby girl named Haya while I was in the hospital. He has been a friend ever since. We discussed matters of mutual interest and concern away from medicine and my health status. I discovered the ingenious innovative mind of both Umair, his son, and himself.

Less than two weeks after I was released from the hospital, although my chest wound had not completely healed, Céline and I flew to Washington on November 14, 2006, along with detailed medical reports to be given to cardiologists and wound specialists upon arrival. It was a heartwarming reception with a combination of tears and smiles when Yasmeen held me tight in her arms in spite of her big belly carrying her baby in the ninth month. Four days later an ecstatic, happy event occurred as we were waiting in a maternity reception area at Sibley hospital when Mark came out announcing for the first time the name of his daughter. With a lot of excitement, he said, "Ashling was just born."

During the four years I taught at SFS-Q, I continued to participate in national, regional and international conferences. One month from my arrival in Qatar, I gave a public lecture to the Academic Bridge Program on September 27, 2005, on "The Invisible Hand & the Price of Oil." Commenting on the assertion of President George W. Bush in his 2006 State of the Union Address, I argued in a public lecture that the United States could not be independent of Middle East oil for at least ten years. When the 2008 financial crisis hit, described by Alan Greenspan, the former Chairman of the Board of the United States Federal Reserve Bank, to be worse than that of the Great Depression of 1929, I gave numerous public lectures and television interviews on the subject in which I predicted that unemployment in the United States would rise to ten percent. It did one year later.

When I decided to retire in the spring semester of 2009 for the second time, four years after I arrived in Qatar, I sent the following farewell to all my SFS-Q students, colleagues and staff:

> As I am winding down a lifetime teaching career since 1961 in the United States and retiring for the second time after

having been asked by Dean James Reardon-Anderson to join his mission in Qatar in 2005, I look back at the experience of SFS-Q with fascination and with a deep sense of accomplishment for having been one of its pioneers. It was not only teaching and being active in the work of the different committees I served on, but also I was engaged in a wide range of involvement with a community I've known well for the last thirty-five years. My frequent television appearances on Al-Jazeera, both the Arabic and English channels, BBC, CNN and others, in addition to my public lectures at think tanks such as Georgetown University Center for Regional and International Studies, the Brookings in Doha, the Academic Bridge Program in Qatar Foundation, the University of Sohar and the Chamber of Commerce in Oman, Kuwait University, University of Bahrain, and Dubai School of Government, have all been gratifying as the name of my beloved institution Georgetown University, at which I served on its faculty or else on its Board of Regents since 1967, has been flying high, reflecting its old tradition of excellence and contributions to education. Yet, the enthusiasm I see well expressed on the faces of every incoming class, the last of which I attended on April 18, 2009, at the LAS building, and the eagerness for another leap into their future with determination, hopes and new aspiration is genuinely refreshing and therefore can never be forgotten.

The first reply I received was a handwritten note from Jim Reardon-Anderson on the last day of his tenure as dean after four illustrious years and before returning to the main campus as a professor of Chinese studies.

Ib.,
SFS-Q has succeeded in its initial foundation, because of you and your commitment to our school and our students. Your many contributions to this enterprise will be there for all to see and to admire as long as Georgetown remains.
Best,
Jim

A few days after the academic year was over, ending with the graduation, in May 2009, of the first class SFS-Q admitted and I taught in 2005, I returned back home in Kensington. Céline had flown home one week earlier. It was a joy to have come back from my first retirement to continue the sacred mission of education for four years. It was also a joy to have retired for the second time.

During my four-year residency in Qatar there were several highlights. At the commencement of the first class we admitted in August 2005, I had the honor of meeting the Emir Sheikh Hamad and his wife Sheikha Mozah. There were other occasions in which I met with them separately or together. But following my TV interview analyzing the financial crisis of 2008, my student Abdullah, a son of the Emir, contacted me to inform me that the Emir wanted to meet with me. We spent a full hour together after discussing the world economic situation. I was deeply touched when the Emir accompanied me all the way to Abdullah's car. His modesty in addition to his remarkable achievements during his ruling of Qatar since 1995 had immensely impressed me. His wise and innovative leadership made Qatar a focal attention of the world. Doha became a center for international, national and regional conferences at its several five-star hotels such as Doha Sheraton, Four Seasons, Intercontinental, Ritz Carlton and many other well-known hotels. In the last year of my residency in Qatar, I was invited to attend two major summit meetings: an Arab-Summit and the Summit for Arab-South American Countries within few days from one another.

Just as I was putting the last touches on this book, it was announced on December 2, 2010, that Qatar won its bid to host the FIFA world cup in 2022. Besides Qatar, there were other formidable competitors, Australia, Japan, South Korea, and the United States. Through the dedication of my former student Mohammed Al-Thani, who prepared an excellent file for the bid, and his relentless efforts with the full backing of his parents, the Emir and Sheikha Mozah as well as his brother Sheikh Tamim, the Heir Apparent, and a dedicated team well chosen for the challenge, Qatar became the winner.

I met with Mohammed at the Four Seasons in Doha after his graduation from Georgetown University School of Foreign Service in Qatar. I could easily detect in our conversation his ultimate dedication to win the bid. This event will certainly add to the economic growth of Qatar even beyond the year 2022 and will have a multiplier effect not only inside the country but regionally and internationally. It will create new jobs for workers and experts from the furthest corners of the world. Only a few days following the good news for Qatar, I flew to Doha to participate in the three-day World Innovation Summit for Education (WISE) held on December 7-9, 2010, to witness the national festivities. It was an opportunity to congratulate Sheikha Mozah personally. I said, "It is a pride for all Arabs, whether they are Egyptians, Moroccans, Saudis or all others, what Qatar has achieved."

4

Beyond the Classroom

Throughout my teaching career, I have always been involved in research, writing, and participating in academic and other conferences as well as in consultations. In preparing my research papers, I spent countless hours in the stacks, both at university libraries and at the Library of Congress, especially after I accepted a teaching position at Georgetown. I have always been proud of my contributions to the larger world of scholars and policymakers. Here are some of the stories that are most notable.

An interesting story worth telling was that of *petrodollars*, one of the several terms I coined. In the war of October 6, 1973, also known as the Yum Kippur War, Egypt was able militarily to cross the Suez Canal and destroy the most fortified line in the history of warfare. Since the June 5, 1967 war, known as the Six-Day War, when Israel attacked Egypt under the one-eyed General Moshe Dayan and occupied the entire Sinai using Egypt's economic resources to the benefit of an otherwise stagnating Israeli economy, Egypt had been using all diplomatic means to have Israel withdraw from Egyptian territories. Despite all of its efforts and UN Security Council Resolution 242, Israel turned a deaf ear. The United States sided—as usual—with Israel in spite of the fact that it was against American interests in the long run. Egypt's ruler Gamal Abdel Nasser started a war of attrition but to no avail, while Israel kept using Egypt's oil and touristic areas around Mount Sinai, in addition to the development of the much-sought-after resort of Charm-el-Sheikh at the southern tip of the Sinai Peninsula.

After Nasser's death in late 1970, President Anwar Sadat

assumed Egypt's leadership. He was little known in the West. Roland Evans invited me to lunch at the Metropolitan Club on 17th Street, close to the White House. He was a prominent syndicated columnist whose articles were published in the *Washington Post* among other newspapers. He asked me, "Who is Anwar Sadat?" I told him a political joke that had just surfaced when he became president. Egyptians are known for expressing their frustrations, real political beliefs and true sentiments through jokes that fly quickly by word of mouth to the furthest corners of Egypt in no time, in coffee shops, clubs, social gatherings, work-places, friends and others. It was known that President Nasser asked his secret service to report to him some political jokes that expressed the true feelings of the people he was ruling.

The joke went as follows:

President Sadat was riding the presidential limousine for the first time after having assumed office when the driver turned his head asking as he was approaching an intersection.

"Mr. President," the driver asked, "shall I turn right or left?"

Sadat answered: "Which way did President Nasser— may God bless his soul—use to take?"

"He used to take the left road," the driver responded (symbolizing the Soviet Union).

"All right, put on the left signal and turn right," Sadat quickly replied.

As he was sipping his favorite drink, Rolly (as I called him) asked, "Do you think that the new president of Egypt will shift the country's orientation from the left bloc towards the West, in particular the United States?" My answer was in the affirmative and my prediction turned out to be right.

Soon after, Sadat ordered the return of all Soviet advisors back home without even asking for anything in return from the United States. He relied heavily on reports from Ashraf Ghorbal, a senior Egyptian diplomat who was the Chief of Egypt's Interests Section in Washington from 1968 until he was recalled to Cairo in 1971 to become Egypt's spokesman. Ashraf and I were bonded for life with lasting friendship until he passed away in 2006, leaving behind an unforgettable legacy in the best of diplomacy and service. In spite of his enormous impact on highly influential people in the United States who had known and respected him since his graduate studies at Harvard University after World War II, Ashraf Ghorbal had to report to President Sadat that diplomacy had no chance to sway the United States from blindly supporting Israel to a fair and peaceful means to return occupied Sinai back to Egypt. In the meanwhile, I had conducted a study on the Israeli economy using Israeli sources at the Near East Section of the Library of Congress. Its head, George N. Atiyeh, and his staff were of tremendous assistance. Later on, we co-edited *Arab Civilization*, a reference book, with each of us authoring one chapter. Having read the study, which concludes that only wars and territorial expansions can keep Israel going, Ashraf Ghorbal showed it to President Sadat and discussed it with him.

That study had a wide circulation. I gave a copy to Prince Bandar bin Sultan who was being treated at Walter Reed Hospital at that time. Every time we met afterwards, he kept reminding me of the lasting impact that study had had on him. Later on, Prince Bandar became an influential Saudi ambassador and the dean of the diplomatic corps in Washington until he returned to Riyadh. I also showed the study to Jeane Kirkpatrick who later became the U.S. ambassador to the United Nations during the Reagan administration. Even if her sentiments were totally with the Israelis, she could not refute the facts I dug out. Nevertheless, she became furious and discussed it with her class. My office at Nevils Building was broken into with nothing missing except one file that contained all the information I collected for the study. Maybe one of her students shared her antagonism against the study and decided to bury it.

With all the reports President Sadat received, including my study, he had courageously decided that the only way to peace is to go to war. After recapturing Sinai, he would negotiate for peace from a point of strength. The lightning victory of the Egyptian forces had caught the world attention and destroyed the myth of the omnipotent Israeli military superiority. The body of my 21-year old nephew, First Lieutenant Fouad Oweiss, was found three miles behind the Israeli lines on the first day of the war on October 6, 1973.

The Egyptian-Israeli tank battle in the Sinai was the largest in the history of warfare. Egypt triumphed. The Israeli commander Assaf was taken prisoner until he was released and returned to Israel. Having been preoccupied with the Watergate scandal that eventually led to his resignation, President Nixon left the matter to the then–Secretary of State, Henry Kissinger. It was the latter who decided to build a bridge of military support to Israel no matter what the cost. The rationale given by him was that he would not allow Soviet weapons used by Egypt to defeat those the Americans supplied abundantly to the Israelis. I was an eyewitness to a newly manufactured American tank that had only 12 miles on the odometer after it was flown into the Sinai. It was captured by the Egyptians and went into display at the Gezira Museum in Cairo where I saw it on my first trip to Egypt on November 20, 1973, after the war. The word victory in Arabic, *Al-Nasr*, was inscribed on the wall behind it.

Through its satellites flying high over the battlefield, the United States government informed Israel that there was a gap between Egypt's second and third armies. The Israelis exploited this information skillfully. They moved quickly to cross east of the Suez Canal into the western province of Sharqia not far from Cairo. Even though it seemed that there were two winners of the war, yet if Egypt wanted to annihilate the Israeli army at high cost of human casualties, it could have been able to do it swiftly. Had it happened, it would have taken years for Israel to rebuild its army. Henry Kissinger flew to Egypt mainly to save the Israeli army but under the disguise of disengagement from war, to which Egypt and Israel had finally agreed.

The Unites States' siding with Israel had ignited disbelief and anger in the Arab world from the Atlantic Ocean to the Arabian Gulf, both from governments and the people. Demonstrations which erupted against the United States expressed the feelings of the Arabs wherever they were. Another reaction was the announcement of a policy of Arab oil boycott in October 1973 against the United States and other allies of Israel. It has prompted what is known as the first shock when the price of oil was quadrupled effective January 1, 1974. The Arab oil embargo would not have had any impact on the flow of oil for two reasons: oil tankers loaded with oil had already left the Arab territorial waters and by the time they reached their destinations to supply oil to refineries in the west the Arab oil embargo had been lifted. Even though the embargo was too short to have any effect on the United States, a substantial reduction in the supply of gasoline was felt from coast to coast leading to price spikes and long lines of cars at gasoline stations.

U.S. major oil companies exploited the psychological impact of the so-called Arab oil embargo to their ultimate benefit. They intentionally reduced the supply of gasoline at their refineries in order to put pressure on the U.S. government to lift its regulations on oil prices, because national oil producers in the U.S. were not allowed to increase the price of what was known as the "old oil." The strategy worked. Oil prices were deregulated creating windfall profits for the U.S. oil companies. Long lines at the gas pumps, on the one hand, and the quadrupling of the price of oil on the other, became the major concerns and monopolized media headlines. As an oil economist, I was interviewed on major networks and was invited to lecture on the subject.

In planning for its March 1974 annual conference, the Committee for Monetary Research and Education (CMRE), one of the many think tanks in the United States, thought of inviting Ali El-Greitly, a former professor of mine in 1949 at King Farouk University, a leading and highly respected economist from Egypt, to address the subject of oil. Instead of traveling all the way from Cairo to New York, Ali El-Greitly suggested my name. In the meanwhile Shaker Khayatt, a banker in New York contacted his primary-school classmate, Ambassador Ashraf Ghorbal, seeking his opinion. Ashraf gave his strong endorsement of Dr. El-Greitly's recommendation. Upon receiving an invitation from CMRE, I traveled to the conference location, Arden House, a big mansion owned and managed by Columbia University for educational meetings. It was built on the highest point on Orama Mountain with a breathless view of the Hudson Highlands in all directions. The road going upward around the mountain from its main gate to the mansion was five miles. Incidentally, my roommate was Austin Colgate, a banker from New York and a partner of J. William Middendorf, who later became the U.S. Secretary of the Navy in the Ronald Reagan administration in the 1980s.

The CMRE is an independent think tank devoted to a return to the gold standard. Many of its members were influenced by the famous Austrian economist Ludwig von Mises, who deprecated the idea that only governments can take a commodity such as paper, splash it with ink, and call it money. Hence it is not the price of goods and services that keeps increasing; it is the purchasing power of paper money that keeps falling. Von Mises had a significant influence on the modern libertarian movement. In fact there is a Ludwig von Mises Institute in Auburn Alabama with a multitude of educational programs and activities.

The theme of the CMRE conference I addressed was "The World Monetary Crisis." Many notable economists, thinkers, and writers gathered in the conference auditorium at Arden House. They included Nicholas Deak, a banker and one of the wealthiest people in the United States, John Exter, a senior vice president of Citibank, Elizabeth Currier, an efficient administrator, J. William Middendorf, a prominent banker along with his partner Austin Colgate, and economists Norman Bailey, Henry Hazlitt, Karl Wiegand, Howard Segermark and Don Kemmerer. Also in attendance was Leonard Silk, a well-known *New York Times* staff writer.

The presentation of my paper entitled "Petrodollars: Problems and Prospects" was in the afternoon of the first day of March 1974. I argued the price of oil was kept low by design of the seven major international oil companies, four American and three European, owning the vast majority of the oil in the world, for two reasons. Since the royalties they paid to the governments where oil was extracted was a fraction of the price, the lower the oil price the less the royalty they paid. The second reason was that those seven sisters sold oil at low prices to their own refineries and downstream operations, thus reaping windfall profits throughout the period of oil concessions. While the price of oil was kept at $1.80 a barrel for many years, prices of other goods and services had been increasing.

I mentioned that in 1973, world attention was once again directed toward the subject of oil, not only as an economic factor but also in terms of political, historical, social, strategic, engineering and other technical dimensions. It was evident that the main focus was on the Middle East as the geographic area with the largest known reserves in the world.

Since the beginning of the 1970s, events had all pointed the way to a structural change in the price of oil, which had been held to almost the same level since the end of World War II. Furthermore, with the independence of several Gulf countries and as a result of a multitude of historical and political developments, there were indications of an inevitable shift in the ownership of Middle East oil from the major Western international oil companies to the governments of the oil exporting nations. As a result of such developments, oil-exporting nations, the majority of which were Third World countries, anticipated substantial increases in their oil reserves. In the meanwhile, advanced industrialized nations of the West and Japan became more dependent than ever on the supply of oil emanating largely from members of the Organization of Petroleum Exporting Countries.

The revolutionary oil era of the 1970s was unique in the history of Third World countries. It required an innovative approach and a new terminology. I moved on to explain the term I coined. "Petrodollars" may be defined as U.S. dollars earned from the sale of oil, or they may be simply defined as oil revenues denominated in U.S. dollars. Petrodollars accrued to oil-exporting nations depend on the sale price of oil as well as the volume being sold abroad, which is in turn dependent on oil production. The overall world supply of oil, on the one hand, and the world demand, on the other, will determine sooner or later an actual market price for oil regardless of any administered pricing system. A price proclaimed by OPEC can be maintained only so long as there is sufficient demand to absorb the amount being supplied in world markets. If demand exceeds supply, oil will be sold at an even higher price than that determined by OPEC. The opposite holds true when an oil glut occurs. This is reflected in a drop in the price after a certain time lag regardless of the price dictated by OPEC. The experience of the 1970s is no more than an application of microeconomic tools to the pricing of oil in world markets.

"Petrodollar surpluses" may also be defined as the net U.S. dollars earned from the sale of oil that are in excess of internal development needs. Petrodollar surpluses, accrued in the process of converting subsoil wealth into an internal income-generating capital stock, refer to oil production that exceeds such needs but is transformed into monetary units. Since petrodollars and petro-dollar surpluses are by definition denominated in U.S. dollars, then purchasing power is dependent on the U.S. rate of inflation and the rate at which the U.S. dollar is exchanged (whenever there is a need for convertibility) by other currencies in international money markets. It follows that whenever economic or other factors affect the U.S. dollar, petrodollars will be affected in the same magnitude. The link, therefore, between the U.S. dollar and petrodollar surpluses, in particular, has significant economic, political, and other implications.

First, the placement of petrodollar surpluses of the Arab-oil exporting nations in the United States may be regarded politically as "hostage capital." In the event of a major political conflict between the United States and an Arab oil-exporting nation, the former with all its military power can confiscate or freeze these assets or otherwise limit their use. It can impose special regulations or at least use regulations for a time in order to attain certain political, economic, or other goals. It may be argued that such actions are un-American, since they are a direct violation of the sacred principles of capitalism and economic freedom. Nevertheless, the U.S. government resorted to such weapons twice in the 1980s against Iranian and Libyan assets. It follows, therefore, that governments placing their petrodollar surpluses in the United States may lose part of their economic and political independence. Consequently, the more petrodollar surpluses are placed in the United States by a certain oil-exporting nation, the less independent such a nation becomes.

Second, an oil-exporting country can have petrodollar surpluses only if its absorptive capacity is less than its earnings from the sale of oil for any particular period of time. It follows, therefore, that petrodollar surpluses depend on oil prices, quantities exported, and the nation's absorptive capacity.

Third, petrodollar surpluses do not represent real wealth but rather are a vehicle by which the latter can be acquired. If kept in liquid form such as paper dollars, their purchasing power will gradually be eroded by inflation and adverse foreign exchange rates. Both are affected in the United States by a host of variables, for example, money supply, interest rates, marginal productivity, stage of a business cycle, and balance-of-payments deficit. Also a factor is U.S. monetary and fiscal policy which in turn affects some of these variables. Furthermore, changes in the U.S. laws and regulations have an impact on the economic variables, which may affect inflation rates and foreign exchange rates. Thus, the purchasing power of liquid petrodollar surpluses belonging, for example, to Arab oil-exporting nations is determined by a complicated set of variables whose trends and quantities are a function of' factors that are not in the control of these countries.

Fourth, efficient allocation of petrodollars for internal investments could increase the productive capacity of an oil-exporting nation and may work to its relative advantage. However, dependency on imported consumer goods, including luxury and rare collector's items, promotes the export of limited resources that could have been otherwise used for internal capital development.

Fifth, the economic development of an oil-exporting nation is based on the conversion of its subsoil resources into other assets such as industrial plants, equipment, education, technology, infrastructure, and other forms of real wealth, that is, real capital stock. Obviously the conversion process can be carried on at different rates. An optimum rate is achieved when oil is pumped at a level that can maximize the present discounted value of the income created in the conversation process. By pumping oil in excess of an optimum production rate, countries such as Saudi Arabia, Kuwait, Qatar, the United Arab Emirates, and others accumulated petrodollar surpluses until 1981. It is worth noting that the difference between the volume of oil actually supplied and the volume that should have been supplied in observance of standard microeconomic theory is in fact a subsidy granted, in real terms, to oil-importing nations such as the United States, Germany, France, and Japan.

I then discussed the allocation of petrodollar surpluses. I explained that the bulk was held either in U.S. treasury bills and other short-term instruments or in American and Western European banks. An examination of balance sheets of banks operating in Saudi Arabia, Kuwait, Qatar, Bahrain, the United Arab Emirates, and Oman revealed that most of their monetary assets were deposited in foreign banks in Europe and the United States. Petrodollar surpluses had also been used to increase the official reserves of the oil-exporting countries at both the International Monetary Fund and the International Bank for Reconstruction and Development. Petrodollar surpluses had been recycled by commercial banks in the United States and other industrialized nations as well as by international institutions. By drawing against petrodollar surpluses as deposits or certificates of deposits, banks were able to expand their volume of lending. For bankers the most obvious clients were the developing countries, mainly in Latin America, such as Mexico, Brazil, and Argentina.

The process of petrodollar recycling makes it possible for commercial banks of industrialized nations, international lending institutions, and Arab banking consortia to provide financial assistance to less-developed countries (LDCs). Western Europe, Japan, and the United States buy oil from oil-exporting countries (OECs). LDCs pay for oil imports and other foreign goods and services with money borrowed from Western commercial banks. The process of recycling is complete when those commercial banks and institutions obtain cash and investments from OECs.

Petrodollar surpluses have also contributed to the growth of the Euromoney market, which was treated by the Soviet Union in the 1950s, when it opened a dollar account in London. Its purpose was to protect the Soviets from a U.S. freeze on their deposits, which could happen if such deposits were placed in the United States. Prior to the first oil shock of 1973, the main source of Eurodollars was the U.S. balance-of-payments deficits. These grew from $17 billion in 1964 to $96 billion in 1970. Additionally, several regulations set by the U.S. Department of the Treasury discouraged American multinational corporations from repatriating profits from overseas operations; thus, these deposits remained in Europe and served as a source of international finance. In 1971, U.S. balance-of-payments deficits suddenly tripled, thus precipitating a huge leap in dollar holdings in foreign banks that led to a massive expansion of money supplies in member countries of the Organization of Economic Cooperation and Development (OECD). In my opinion, this was one of the main causes of the leap in the rate of inflation and the economic disequilibrium that came long before the rise in the price of oil at the end of 1973. Contrary to the fear that the quadrupling of the price of oil by the end of 1973 would ruin the international monetary system, I argued the exact opposite. As it turned out, it created new markets, increased trade, and recycled money.

The following is a part from my study that I presented in March 1974 and was subsequently published in the *New York Times* in an article edited by Leonard Silk:

I am restricting my remarks to petrodollars of Arab oil-exporters since they have the largest known reserves of oil in the world and since they are the largest exporters of this vital commodity.

As a wealth holder, the Arab oil-producing countries ought to have at least the following goals: 1. portfolio management, 2. minimization of risks of holding foreign money in foreign markets, 3. economic development of the Arab world.

In pursuing the first two goals, American and European financial institutions together with Arab banks formed the following multinational combines:

Union de Banques Arabes et Françaises (UBAF) established in Paris in 1970 with more than $700 million in assets. It is 40% owned by Credit Lyonnais but controlled by fourteen Arab Banks with 60% share. UBAF has subsidies in London, Rome, Frankfurt, Luxembourg, and Tokyo. Partners of those subsidiaries include several big European banks and the Bank of Tokyo.

Banque Franco-Arabe d' Investissements Internationaux (FRAB) which was chartered in Paris in 1969 by the Kuwait Investment Company in partnership with the French Société Generale and the Société de Banque Suisse. It has about $180 million in assets.

The European Arab Bank, which was started in 1972, headquartered in Luxemburg, and was made up of 16 Arab Financial institutions including (FRAB) and seven European banks. It has subsidiaries in Brussels and Frankfurt and plans branches in Paris and Milan.

La Compagnie Arabe et Internationale d'Investissement which was incorporated in Luxembourg in January 1973. It is owned by 24 Arab and Western banks including the Bank of America together with West German, Italian, Japanese and French banks. It opened its first subsidiary in April 1973 in Paris.

In addition to those four major consortia, there are several other institutions and banks which are presently competing independently for business among oil-exporting Arab countries. First National City Bank of New York operated branches in Beirut, Saudi Arabia, Bahrain and Dubai. Chase Manhattan Bank of New York has branches in Beirut and in Bahrain. Chase Manhattan along with Morgan Guaranteed Trust of New York holds most of Saudi Arabian government deposits. In addition, a number of American banks operate out of Beirut, which is regarded as Mideast financial center. There is only one private Arab institution, the Arab Bank, which is functioning on an international basis bidding for Arab money. The Arab Bank is incorporated by Abdel-Meguid Shouman in Jordan and has branches in Zurich, London and Frankfurt. It plans to open a branch in New York City.

In concluding my presentation, I gave advice to Saudi Arabia that, as the country with the largest reserves, it should denominate the price of its oil in units of gold but payable in U.S. dollars, depending on the prevailing rate of exchange. I argued that other oil-exporting nations may follow suit, thus oil prices may be stabilized over time. I received a flattering standing ovation after my presentation. I was equally flattered when Georgetown University School of Foreign Service in Qatar, surprised me with a design of a mock "petrodollar bill" commissioned especially on the occasion of my retirement on May 8, 2009.

Following my presentation at the conference of the Committee for Monetary Research and Education at Arden House on March 1, 1974, and Leonard Silk's article in the *New York Times*, the term petrodollar has been known worldwide ever since. I was interviewed on major television networks in the United States and abroad on different subjects related to petrodollars and the international financial implications. Following the media coverage of my presentation at Arden House, I was invited by the League of Arab States to address its Ninth Congress held in Dubai at the Intercontinental hotel just opened for the occasion. I had an audience with the ruler, Sheikh Rashid Al-Maktoum, who wanted to seek my advice on investments. My reply was gold and real estate. It was free advice but Dubai gained substantial profits as the price of gold kept increasing. In his majestic reception area, I noticed the largest one-piece Persian rug that I had ever seen specifically woven for the spacious area.

I had also received a call from Ardachir Zahedi, then the ambassador of Iran to the United States, asking if he can drop by my apartment for a few minutes. He brought with him a bag of Persian pistachios with a verbal personal message of appreciation from the Shah of Iran. He invited me to a reception at the uniquely designed Embassy with its mosaic façade on Massachusetts Avenue, where I met his lady companion at the time who happened to be a famous movie star, the stunningly beautiful Elizabeth Taylor.

In January 1975 I was asked to give a seminar on petrodollar allocations to a group of British Petroleum senior executives at Britannica House in London on a Thursday morning. I had a morning class at Georgetown University on Wednesday, the day before, and a senior seminar in the afternoon on Thursday. I made it. After the morning class, I drove to Dulles Airport, left my car in its spacious parking lot and boarded the British Concorde at noon, arriving in London at 9:00 p.m. A chauffeur in a silver Rolls Royce picked me up directly to have a conversation with the Chairman of the Board, Sir Eric Drake, and a late snack with him.

He gave me an illustrative book on BP's history, one which I already knew well. The company was established in 1909 as the Anglo-Persian Oil Company, few years after William Knox D'Arcy was granted an oil concession by the Shah of Iran in May 1901 to search for oil, which he discovered in 1908. In 1954, it changed its name to British Petroleum, and in 2000 it merged with Amoco and ARCO. It is the largest corporation in the United Kingdom, the third largest global energy company, and the fourth largest company in the world. Its revenues exceed the entire gross domestic product of Egypt.

The company's influence with the British and the American governments allowed it to save itself from the early Iranian nationalization of its oil resources, as planned by the country's strong prime minister, Dr. Mohammad Mosaddegh. In June 1953, the Eisenhower administration approved a British proposal for a joint Anglo-American operation, code-named Operation Ajax, to overthrow Mosaddegh. Kermit Roosevelt, of the United States Central Intelligence Agency (CIA), traveled secretly to Iran to coordinate plans with the shah and the Iranian military, which was led by General Fazlollah Zahedi.

In talking with Sir Eric Drake, I got to admire him not only for heading and managing a multinational empire but also because of his keen interest in and support of education. The following day, after my presentation, I had conversations with those in attendance among the top executives of British Petroleum from 9:00 to 11:30 a.m. at Britannica House. Then, I was driven to Terminal 3 at Heathrow Airport and had enough time to enjoy drinks and snacks in the Concorde Lounge. The supersonic airplane departed at 1:00 p.m. flying at 60,000 feet high where I could clearly see the curvature of the earth on Mach 2. It arrived at Dulles Airport at noon; with the time zone change, it was one hour earlier than the time the airplane took off from London. I drove my car to Georgetown, arriving ahead of time to meet my senior seminar on the same day. It was the fastest trip I had ever made across the Atlantic, enabling me to meet my classes on time on two executive days and to fulfill my obligation to British Petroleum in London in between.

Following the second oil shock in 1979–80, I advised Sheikh Ahmed Zaki Yamani, the Minister of Petroleum in Saudi Arabia, at a meeting in Geneva, Switzerland, to use his influence at an OPEC meeting to reduce the price of oil from the high price it was recorded at $34 a barrel to $12 at a time when there was a glut on international oil markets, i.e., when there was more supply of oil than demand at the high price. At an OPEC meeting, it was decided to reduce the oil price to $27. With the continued glut, market forces kept decreasing the oil price as determined by supply and demand at the New York Mercantile Exchange until it reached by the late nineteen eighties less than $10 a barrel.

In the meanwhile, I was asked to present my views at Oxford University's St. Anthony's College on November 12, 1982. I introduced a new tool of economic analysis showing that the conventional downward sloping of demand—concave to the origin—had to be adjusted. I argued that when the price goes up, the demand may hardly be reduced, but as it keeps climbing, eventually demand is reduced, hence the upward price cycle would be convex to the origin until a high price would have dual effects, a reduction in demand and an increase in supply as it becomes economical for marginal oil wells to produce at high prices. Such force will have to push the oil price downwardly according to the conventional demand curve. But to clear the market, the price would need to be drastically reduced. My analysis, therefore, predicted in 1982 that the oil price will be significantly reduced, and my predictions in this regard turned out to be true. The tool of analysis I introduced was published in *Blakely's Commodity Review* on May 1, 1983, under the title "The Oweiss Demand Curve." The last speech I gave at the conference of the Committee for Monetary Research and Education (CMRE) held at the Union League Club in New York City was in 2002. I shared the podium with the Nobel Prize-winner in Economics, Robert Mundell addressing the euro versus the U.S. dollar in 2002.

Four notable friends emerged out of my participations at CMRE. They were Bill Middendorf, Nicholas Deak, John Exter, and Norman Bailey, all of whom I met for the first time at Arden House at the beginning of March 1974.

John William Middendorf II
   John William Middendorf II, a tall, refined gentleman, rushed towards me after my presentation to shake hands, congratulating me for what he termed "a superb contribution to CMRE." During the two-day meeting, we had several conversations to get to know one another. He even offered me a ride, in a car he rented, to La-Guardia Airport. In addition to being a diplomat and a prominent investment banker together with Austin Colgate, he informed me of his interests in antiques, the arts and music both playing and composing. In fact, when he was appointed the U.S. ambassador to the Netherlands in the Nixon administration, his gift to the Dutch Queen was a symphony he composed and named "The Holland Symphony." He also composed other symphonies and fifty marches.
   In addition to being a prolific composer, he was also a prominent member of the Republican Party and served on the Republi-

can National Committee. I introduced him to Ashraf Ghorbal, the dynamic Egyptian ambassador to the United States. The two men hit well with one another after they both discovered they attended Harvard University. Ghorbal urged him to go to Egypt to oversee the role of the U.S. Navy in removing all obstacles and war debris from the Suez Canal after the 1973 October War to make it navigable once again. It had been blocked since Israel waged its war in 1967 denying Egypt one of the main sources of foreign exchange from tolls collected from passing ships in the vital waterway. His gift to President Sadat was a march he named the "Suez Canal." As a result, the Egyptian Merit Decoration First Order was conferred upon him.

We met at least once a year at Arden House for the annual CMRE conference. We saw one another often, particularly when he moved to Washington to head the Financial General Bankshares, a block away from the White House. We always had intellectually stimulating conversations and I found him to be a brilliant innovative thinker. No wonder he was one of the architects of the North America Free Trade Agreement. He had a remarkable record in deepening economic cooperation and trade relations as the U.S. Permanent Representative to the Organization of American States.

He came to me once asking if Ghorbal could put a good word on his behalf with the Secretary of Defense, James Schlesinger, who had known him well since Harvard. Bill wanted to be promoted from Undersecretary of the Navy, the position he assumed since October 1974, to Secretary of the Navy. We were all delighted when he was appointed to the position he desired. On such a memorable occasion, I held a black tie dinner in his honor. Several ambassadors and prominent personalities attended.

I had the distinct pleasure of nominating him for the distinguished National Bank of Egypt Commemorative Lecture Program in Cairo. Since it started in 1950, several prominent world thinkers including Friedrich A. Hayek, William Lewis, Gottfried Haberler, Bent Hansen, and Walter Rostow addressed it, some of whom were Nobel Prize winners such as Gunnar Myrdal. In 1979, J. William Middendorf II gave an innovative lecture entitled "An Economic Alliance in the Red Sea." A sad event occurred when he was in Egypt. His wife called me asking how she could contact him in

Cairo following the death of their daughter. Céline and I among hundreds of friends, acquaintances, and relatives attended a memorial service at a church on Massachusetts Avenue to share their grief and to offer our condolences to our esteemed friends. I was later invited to give a lecture in the same series. The title of my presentation was "The Underground Economy with Special Reference to the Case of Egypt" on December 19, 1994, in which I estimated Egypt's hidden economy to be almost equal to the official figure of the country's gross domestic product. Throughout our years of friendship, he never seized to amaze me with his deep thoughts and analysis on all national and international developments and concerns.

Nicholas L. Deak

Nicholas L. Deak asked me to join him at his table in the elaborate dining room of Arden House on March 1, 1974. Even though he was almost as old as my father, a friendship emerged until he died tragically on November 18, 1985.

He was an internationally known banker who had built an empire of foreign exchange businesses around the free world. We had many encounters either at his Scarsdale mansion with its three-mile track enabling him to run on his own property every day, or at conferences where we were both speakers. In spite of his almost seventy years of age, he had the energy and health of a young man. He used to run three miles every day even on his frequent travels. Nick and his Viennese wife Lisl used to go on skiing trips in the best-known resorts. In dining with him, I noticed how strictly he adhered to his vegetarian diet.

On a cold day of January 1984, at his office in the skyscraper carrying his own name in downtown New York, he informed me that he and his wife wished to go back to Egypt but only if Céline and I were to be traveling with them. As a man with diversified commitments, he had his schedule planned for two years in advance. I suggested December of the same year, upon which he called on his secretary to cancel or postpone his appointments for the ten days we agreed on, while I was admiring the panoramic view of New York harbor from his spacious office on one of the top floors of his skyscraper.

On our trip to Egypt, we took a tour of Luxor, Aswan, Mount Sinai, and the Red Sea resort areas. Mrs. Jehan Sadat invited us at the home of former President Sadat by the Nile River. In Aswan, we visited an impressive Philae temple on an island in the middle of the Nile River. The guide kept explaining how those gigantic high walls and columns were constructed, but we were overwhelmed by the sight and preferred to look rather than to listen to him. I arranged for a meeting with the newly appointed Minister of Economy, Mustafa Yousry. As usual, Nick voiced his opinion by saying, "Why are you still messing up your economy by continuing to have a fixed exchange rate of your currency?"

A few months after we returned from that trip, Céline and I were watching the 6:30 news and listening to our favorite TV anchorman Walter Cronkite when we were spellbound seeing the body of Nicholas Deak being carried after he had been fatally shot. The mass media covered the tragic ending of a friend. The *New York Times* reported that his assailant, Lois Lang, "had been arrested at least five times in the Seattle area since 1982 and had once tried to wrest a gun from a police officer. The woman charged with murdering the head of the Deak-Perera foreign-exchange company and a receptionist in Manhattan was released from a mental hospital last August in Washington State, law-enforcement officials said yesterday." As it turned out, she went to New York, purchased a gun and headed for the Deak Building. She took the elevator up to his office suite while a guard left his post for a few minutes. The woman who dreamt she was a part owner of the company asked the receptionist for Mr. Deak, but before she could answered she shot her. Upon hearing a gun shot, Nick, as brave as he had been all of his life, got out of his office facing a strange woman. She shot him dead.

The news was reported worldwide. Mrs. Sadat called me from Egypt asking me to convey her deep condolences to his wife Lisl. Upon contacting Lisl, knowing how strong our friendship had turned out to be, she asked me to eulogize her husband on November 21, 1985, at All Souls Church on Lexington Avenue in New York. I did so before the overflowing crowd:

In mourning Nicholas Deak, we all feel the loss of a giant. The tragedy of his departure not only has shocked his family, his friends and the world, but has placed him among the great men I know.

My first encounter with the Deaks was at Arden House in New York when he invited me to have dinner at his table. As I entered the dining room, I noticed him sitting straight at the head of the table. I felt as though I was in the presence of the type of nobility you only read about in history books but rarely meet.

His strong personality amazed me,

His pertinent questions challenged me,

His wit and sense of humor intrigued me,

His quick remarks fascinated me and

His distinguished character overwhelmed me.

He made you earn his friendship after his microscopic, thorough investigation.

Over the years, a strong bond of friendship was built as we met in numerous professional encounters here and abroad. I got to know his remarkable contributions; I considered him a great mentor of mine. The frequency of our meetings not only deepened our friendship, but also made me discover, behind his awesome look, his true affection and a genuine, kind and tender heart.

When my wife and I spent some time vacationing in Egypt with Nick and Lisl, we were all amazed at his constant quest for learning about a culture and a history he was not very familiar with. In those memorable weeks shortly after Christmas in 1983, he was always intriguing, always inspiring, always questioning, and always ahead of us in thinking and in action. He jogged around the pyramids at seven o'clock in the morning. In January, he swam in the Mediterranean Sea, off the coast of El-Arish, while the temperature was forty degrees Fahrenheit. In short, there was not a single dull moment around him.

As we were driving in the Sinai desert at night, surrounded with utter darkness, we stopped for a few moments. He looked up at a sky full of bright stars and was fascinated. Not only because it was an unforgettable scene—as he told me in his deep warm voice—but because he felt he identified with the crystal clarity of those stars. That was the way Nicholas Deak was.

At Luxor's Karnak, he felt the sensation of greatness and immortality as he stood close to those gigantic columns and spectacular colossi. He was overwhelmed by such creation of man at the dawn of history and he identified with that feeling of greatness and immortality.

Nicholas Deak impressed great personalities and world leaders he met throughout his life. Yet he had a unique ability to reach out to simple people through his warmth and affection. Nevertheless, it was an extremely difficult task to keep up with his ingenuity and high standards. Remarkably, his wife Lisl, through her love, dedication and admiration was allowed to affect him because of his greatest respect and love for her.

Nicholas Deak was a perfectionist in whatever he did. Likewise, he did not accept less than perfection from others. This was a source of frustration for him as he dealt with other people. He built an empire in the business world that kept growing and progressing over the years. He was very faithful and appreciative of those who worked for him throughout those years. Yet, in spite of his monumental achievements and all the honors and recognitions he had received, and in spite of being himself a very proud man, he was internally a humble and a modest human being with an enormous reservoir of love and affection which he never spoke of, but his actions reflected the most tender feelings a human being can have. I noticed how much respect, admiration and affection he had for his wife Lisl, his sister Margaret and her family, his son Leslie, his daughter-in-law Robin and his grandchildren, Lindsay, Travis and Amanda. He ran, swam and did gymnastics with them. In the meanwhile, he planted in their minds how to meet a challenge and how to aspire for the very best.

Nicholas Deak was not only a man with unsurpassed experience in practical matters, but he was also an educator and a scholar. His students admired his depth, breadth, and clarity of mind. Being meticulous about details, he never lost track of an overall concept, as an engineer would do when he fits a perfect bolt while building an airplane.

Nicholas Deak wrote extensively and lectured widely around the world. Furthermore, his contributions to education and higher institutions of learning and research were diverse and immense. He was very proud of his distinguished service to the United States which was carried out with outstanding bravery and great affection not only as a Major in World War II, but also in many different assignments and tasks commissioned by several presidents of the United States.

Nicholas Deak was a great advocate of the free economy and a firm believer in the miracle of its efficiency. He dedicated his time, money and energy to restore economic freedom in the land of freedom.

Nicholas Deak will always be a torch to enlighten a successful road to those who wish to follow his giant steps and remarkable achievements. His memory will always be alive in the minds and hearts of all who were fortunate to know him and were close to him.

Turning to the coffin just adjacent to the podium from which I spoke, I looked at his body and said: "Nick, it is impossible to understand this absurdity as to how your life was taken away. It is hard for me to see your body without its dynamism. Nick, I shall miss you forever. May God rest your soul in peace and bestow comfort upon your wife, your sister, your son, and your family."

Ever since, I have been a strong advocate of gun control. Every day in the United States there are cases of homicide mainly in major cities. The ease by which anyone can buy a deadly weapon is astounding. I am a great admirer of Michael Moore who made a superb movie following the Columbine High School massacre on April 20, 1999. Even though the country was shocked when the massacre occurred near Denver, Colorado, yet similar cases happen frequently. Michael was so brave to face up to the strong National Rifle Association (NRA) with its influence through effective lobbying activities and the support of movie stars such as Charlton Heston and politicians such as Sarah Palin for the right to own arms.

John Exter

With enthusiasm John Exter greeted me warmly after my petrodollar presentation. He told me warmly, "Welcome to the club of what I call the great economists of our time." He used to send me his outstanding analysis and predictions until just before he passed away in 2005. John Exter was an internationally respected banker and a firm believer in the gold standard as means of creating a control system over printing paper money. One of his famous quotes he introduced in the mid-1970s reads: "The U.S. and world economies are on the threshold of a deflationary crash that will make the 1930s look like a boom. Gold will be the single best investment to own. Buy it now while it's still cheap." His prediction became utterly true with the 2008 collapse of the financial institutions in the U.S. and the spread of economic recession globally. Building on the fact that a pyramid is one of the most stable structures ever envisioned by humans, he argued that an inverted pyramid is how a debt-based monetary system is constructed.

Logically, an upside-down pyramid implies one of the most "unstable" structures one can imagine. When John Exter constructed his model, the top of the pyramid had junk bonds, failing banks, failing insurance companies, and, we might add, failed investment banks/brokerage houses. Creditors will get out of weak debts and move down the debt pyramid, to the very bottom! Near the bottom we find currency (dollar bills), even though they pay no interest. Next above currency are Treasury bills, issued by the government and backed by the Federal Reserve. They are almost as safe as currency notes, plus they pay interest. However, you have to liquidate the bills to get money of some sort to buy something.

John Exter's reputation and activities went far beyond the territories of the United States. For example, the Central Bank of Sri Lanka recognized the firm foundation he laid for it. In 2007, it renamed its Annual Public Lecture as John Exter Memorial Oration. When I became an ambassador in New York, John Exter nominated me for membership to the prestigious University Club at 54th Street and 5th Avenue. I have kept my membership and paid the annual dues since 1977. It was at that club that Céline and I hosted more than 200 dignitaries including several ambassadors to bid farewell to diplomatic life on November 29, 1978, to return to academia. Of course, John Exter was in attendance. He looked at my wife, and commented to me privately, "She is pregnant like a plum." Indeed, my daughter Yasmeen was born six weeks later.

Norman A. Bailey

Norman Bailey was the only one in the above distinguished group who was my age. I first caught a glimpse of him when he shouted at one of the media correspondents for having interrupted me by posing a second question while I was still answering the first, "Let the professor finish his answer to you." That was the straight-forward man I got to know at Arden House on March 1, 1974. At that time, he was a professor of economics at the City University of New York. His lucid thoughts and his analysis not only in economics but also in politics impressed me. We developed a long-time friendship. It was a pleasure to host him at home while waiting for his confirmation to a key position in the Ronald Reagan adminis-tration. Norman assumed the position of Senior Director of Inter-national Economic Affairs on the National Security Council from 1981 to 1983.

At a family dinner with his wife Suzanne, Norman told us an interesting story of his background. An Armenian living in a small village in Turkey during its conquest and expansion came up with a formula of dried meat called Basterma. The invention helped the Turkish troops to have ample food supplies and facilitated their logistics during the Ottoman Empire domination. The inventor was asked to come to the capital traveling on his donkey to receive the title of Emir, a title passed down by generations to the current holder, who happened to be Norman Bailey, from his ancestral ma-ternal side.

Sir Isaac Newton, one of the great mathematicians in the history of mankind, introduced his famous law: "Every action has a reac-tion, opposite in direction and equal in force." However, in observ-ing actions and reactions throughout history, I may reformulate the law. I would argue that in economics, political events, history, sociology, psychology and all other such fields, the first part could be applicable but not the remainder of the Newton's Law, because in social sciences and humanities *"every action has a reaction"*—not *necessarily opposite in direction and not necessarily equal in force."* In a graduate course I taught, everyone chose an application of what they termed the Newton-Oweiss law following my own interpretation of the far reaching consequences of certain economic actions. The range of reactions in social sciences and humanities may vary from almost no reaction—except probably psychological—to immeasurably large ones. By the same token, every action in the fields of social sciences and the humanities may lead to a variety of reactions in a multiplicity of directions, including, of course, an opposite one.

Numerous applications of the Newton-Oweiss law can be found throughout history. The action of the assassination in Sarajevo on June 28, 1914, of the heir to the Austro-Hungarian throne, Archduke Franz Ferdinand, led to a sequence of a vast array of reactions in World War I, which started exactly one month after the assassination when Austria-Hungary declared war against Serbia. With a multiplicity of treaties, ethnicities and other factors, dozens of countries were drawn to the war: Belgium, Brazil, Bulgaria, Canada, China, Costa Rica, Cuba, Ecuador, France, Germany, Greece, Guatemala, Haiti, Honduras, Italy, Japan, Liberia, Montenegro, New Zealand, Nicaragua, Panama, Peru, Portugal, Romania, Russia, Siam, Turkey, the United Kingdom, the United States, and Uruguay. The devastation of World War I not only affected these counties but also extended to include many other countries and led to worldwide casualties of more than 37 million people.

I also maintain that reactions to past actions are never the same. I think it is a mistake to believe that history repeats itself. There could be some common features that may somewhat be repeated but never exactly in the same way. A tree amongst the incalculable number of trees throughout the world is never the same as any other, even though two trees may share some partial and common features. Every phenomenon around us resembles one of the unlimited variations of trees. It applies to events in history and reactions to actions. Hence, we can never draw conclusions from past experience with certainty, nor can we ever find tailor-made recommendations for what seems to be similar events from the past.

* * *

Although I lived in Egypt until I was 28, I did not get a chance to visit other parts of the Middle East until after I came to live in the United States. While I had been teaching courses in microeconomics, macroeconomics, international trade, statistics, and the course of mathematical economics first introduced by me was added to our curriculum, our chairman, Henry W. Briefs, asked me to teach a selective seminar on Economics of the Middle East. His request sparked me to travel to the region to get fresh information and a feel for its economic conditions.

My first trip the Middle East was in 1971. I flew first from Washington to London to visit my brother Mohamed. Upon arrival, his wife greeted me warmly, telling me that my brother was still in Nigeria to finalize the family's final move to the United Kingdom. She told me that the children were about to come home from the Lycée, the French school in London. They used to ride their bikes in the morning to Surbiton Station and back home after school. It was the first time I had seen Yasin since he was 2 years old and Amr who was six months old when I left Egypt in early 1960. As to the youngest, Yehia, he was born in the Congo in 1963 and thus it was the first highly emotional time that I hugged him. His father had a successful export-import business in Alexandria until Nasser's laws of nationalization in 1961 confiscated it. With his family, he moved to West Africa until he decided it was time for the schooling for his three boys to move to London.

It was an enjoyable four-day visit with my brother's family in the suburbs of London, including a funny story. I invited Ragaa to a musical in London. She gave me Mohamed's car key to drive. It was utterly strange for me to drive on the left side of the road. There was no problem so long as I was driving straight. It was only when I had to turn to another street right or left, I found it awkward. It required too much concentration. We managed. However, on the way back, we lost our way when we were close to home. We pulled to the side where there was a police car. Upon my asking for direction after having given the address, he politely said, "Please follow me, I'll accompany you to your home." Indeed, I found the British police to be very polite. An American neighbor once told me that while in London drinking in a pub, two young men started a quarrel. When two policemen arrived on the scene holding their truncheons, the bartender told them who started it. Two customers sitting at the bar confirmed it. A policeman turned to the offender saying before he handcuffed him, "Sir, I am afraid I have to arrest you."

I traveled from London to Kuwait where I stayed at the Sheraton Hotel. It was the first Sheraton-managed hotel in the world outside of the United States and was owned by the family of the colorful Abdul-Rahman Al-Shaya, known for his great sense of humor and whom I met in Washington when he was a student. I happened to have arrived at a seasonal movement of very thin air blowing from the desert called *Tozz*. It makes visibility very limited, and the thin sand blows through the windowsills. I managed, however, to have my meetings at the Ministry of Economy, the Ministry of Petroleum and the Central Bank through the good offices of my friend Sheikh Salem Al Sabah, who was then the Kuwaiti ambassador to the United States and a prominent member of the ruling family. I gave a lecture at Kuwait University after having gathered economic data about the country and its surrounding neighbors.

I had come to know the diplomatic corps especially of Arab countries because of my keen interest and involvement in economic and international affairs. Sheikh Salem Al Sabah and other Arab ambassadors became close friends of mine. Over a cup of coffee at my apartment in late 1969, I advised Sheikh Salem that in my view the dollar would be devalued. He said, "While I appreciate your advice, I do not know about those economic matters. At the next visit of our Minister of Petroleum, Salem El-Ateeqi, I'll arrange for the three of us to have lunch together at the Embassy."

It was my first acquaintance with the minister. After we finished lunch and sipped our Arabian coffee, the ambassador turned to the minister and said, "I got to know Dr. Oweiss as a highly respected economist. I thought you might be interested to hear his analysis concerning the future of the U.S. dollar."

"The inflation that had swept England necessitated a sharp devaluation of its currency in 1968," I began. "Now, having observed a rise in the rate of inflation in the United States because of overspending on the Vietnam War, unmatched by a reduction in government spending, and a deterioration of its balance of trade, I expect the U.S. dollar to be devalued. The U.S. may resist a devaluation of its currency for awhile because nations usually tie the value of their currencies with national prestige."

"Over my dead body, the dollar will not be devalued," was the minister's answer.

The ambassador interrupted the Minster saying, "Dr. Oweiss is giving his advice free of charge." Observing that I did not wish to continue the meeting with the Minister, the ambassador stood up, shook my hand, and said, "We are indebted to you, Dr. Oweiss, for your valuable advice." Of course, my prognosis turned out to be true. Less than a year from that meeting, the U.S. dollar was devalued twice within a span of fourteen months. No wonder the reception I had had when I visited Kuwait in the aftermath was overwhelming.

From Kuwait, I traveled to Iraq, whose president was Ahmad Hassan al-Bakr until 1979 when Saddam Hussein took his place. Under the philosophy of the Ba'ath renaissance, Iraq allowed any person carrying a passport issued in any of the Arab countries to enter the country without a visa. I was nostalgic to visit *Bilad al-Rafedeen* because of the rich Muslim civilization that had flourished during the European dark ages in this one important center; the other was in Spain, in Cordoba's *Andalus*. Iraq is a rich country with highly educated workers, agriculture resources, and two major rivers, the Tigris and the Euphrates. A prolific British civil servant working in Iraq described the fertility of the land with the following words: "If you tickle its soil, it will smile with a crop." At the Central Bank, I was informed of the country's substantial financial assets that were wiped out later under the regime of Saddam Hussein and his eight-year war against Iran, from 1980 to 1988. I had also an opportunity to give a lecture at its main university and to discuss future economic plans for the country.

From Baghdad, I flew to Jeddah in Saudi Arabia and by car I was driven to Mecca to perform the *Umrah* for the first time. I was overwhelmed spiritually when I prayed at *Al-Kabaa* and completed the full rituals as those of the pilgrimage, except the latter are to be performed at a specific date on the lunar Islamic Calendar. It was only the beginning, to be followed by many other times in later years including the pilgrimage I was blessed to perform in 1990, thus fulfilling the fifth pillar of Islam. I had never counted the numerous times I went for the *Umrah* as each one of them had given me inner tranquility, sanctity and high spiritual devotion to Almighty God in my prayers.

As I stated above, my first glimpse of King Abdel-Aziz was in 1945 during his official visit with King Farouk. I was 13 years old when his open-hooded Rolls Royce traveling at no more than 5 miles an hour passed right in front of us in the royal motorcade. King Farouk, a very beloved monarch at the time, sat with his round face and a big smile next to the one-eyed King Abdel-Aziz who was wearing a typical Saudi head cover. That moving scene was engraved in my memory ever since I was a young boy. I shared that story with Prince Faisal, the eldest son of King Fahd, at a royal dinner he held in Riyadh in honor of four of us: Abdeen Jabbara, a prominent lawyer from Detroit; Hanna Batatu, a well-known scholor who taught at Harvard and at Georgetown University; Sherif Sedky, a top lawyer from the West Coast; and me. Along with words of appreciation, I gave a brief coverage of the subject of an optimum allocation of petrodollars. The visit came about after I was called for a meeting with Prince Faisal, who was the Minister of Youth, during his brief stay in Washington. I was impressed by his knowledge and analysis of international affairs following my answer to his question concerning the allocation of petrodollars. As he wanted to dwell in more details about the subject, he asked me to form a small group under my leadership for a visit to Saudi Arabia. The royal tour included Riyadh, the industrial city of Jbeil, Jeddah, *Umrah* in Mecca and Medina, excluding from the latter part Hanna Batatu because he was not a Muslim. This was one of the many encounters I had with princes of the royal family and some of its prominent ministers, including the colorful Sheikh Ahmed Zaki Yamani, the Minister of Petroleum and Natural Resources, and Hisham Nazer, the Minister of Planning.

Following the dinner, Prince Faisal informed me that he had scheduled a meeting with his father, King Fahd, at 10:00 p.m. Upon arrival shortly before the scheduled time, we were ushered into the King's office. It was small, no larger that the White House Oval Office, with only a small painting hanging on the wall. Our meeting lasted three hours, during which the King spoke lucidly of his grandiose schemes of development, including increasing the volume of water desalination, the expansion of the two Holy Mosques in Mecca and Medina, and of his regional and international concerns. With the inflow of petrodollars, in particular with the first quadrupling of the price of oil as of January 1, 1974, Saudi Arabia embarked on mammoth developmental projects including construction of two industrial cities, Jubeil on the east coast by the Arabian Gulf, and Yanbu on the west coast by the Red Sea. Steve Bechtel, whose company undertook the planning of the two cities, informed me that the project in Jubeil was the largest civil engineering work in the world. Watching the transformation of the country left me breathless.

In June 1976, we were invited to fly to Algeria so I could evaluate its economic performance. We planned a two-month tour. We seized the opportunity to stop in London to introduce my bride to my elder brother Mohamed, his wife Ragaa, and their three sons, Yassin, Amr and Yehia.

Our second stop was Paris where we were received by a high-school classmate of mine, Saad Abu-el-Kheir, who was at the time the deputy chief of the Egyptian Embassy in Paris. Saad and his wife Nadia gave a memorable reception in our honor. We toured the Champs Elysées, the Tuileries Gardens, and Place de la Concorde with its famous Egyptian Obelisk. I took Céline to a small boutique at La Madeleine to choose a couple of fashionable dresses in preparation for her meeting with my family for the first time.

We flew from Paris to Algiers where we were officially greeted. As we were going down the steps, we saw a red carpet being rolled out before we arrived at the last step. High-ranking officials with their wives greeted us warmly saying, "Welcome to the land of Algeria." A large bouquet of flowers was given to Céline. At the end of the red carpet, a black limousine was awaiting for us with all the doors open. We were taken to a special VIP lounge where an official asked us to hand him our passports and the stubs of our suitcases. It was quick. We got our stamped passports back while we were told that our luggage was already in the car.

My task was to evaluate the economic performance of Algeria's industrialization under the rule of President Houari Boumediène. He was the fourth president of Algeria after it gained its independence from France, following a long struggle during which more than one million Algerians out of a total population of six million were killed. With no resources compared to the highly equipped

French army, the Algerians heroically waged street warfare in the Kasbah and in many other locations. At an elaborate dinner at the home of Sadek Guellal, a high-ranking official with the largest economic enterprise in the country, Sonatrach, we learned that several French citizens living in Algeria had joined the Algerians in their struggle against the brutal occupier. His wife was one of them, having been moved by the Algerians' inalienable right to self-determination. President Boumediène ruled the country from 1965 until his death in 1978. Thanks to the natural resources of oil and natural gas in addition to phosphates as another valuable exportable, the government established Sonatrach in 1963 as the national enterprise for research, production, transportation, and commercialization of its hydrocarbon resources. It became a vast empire in its own right as the sole company with multiple and diversified activities in hydrocarbon exploration, extraction, production, refining as well as petrochemical industries and desalination of sea water. Sonatrach contributes to almost one-third of Algeria's gross national product and is one of the eleven largest oil consortiums in the world.

Being left of center, President Boumediène followed the Soviet Union's industrialization policy of self-sufficiency no matter what the cost. In examining the necessary data provided by the different branches of the government, but also based on my visits to the sites of industrial factories, I concluded my report with the high cost of autarky. I found that a governmental tractor factory was working at only five percent of its capacity—and most of the tractors produced were not sold and were left in a huge open space. I asked a sample of farmers for their opinion of the nationally produced tractors, and the answer was that imported foreign ones were superior in performance, in service and in the availability of spare parts. But the Algerian government did not pay enough attention to such economic waste, as its revenues had substantially increased resulting from the quadrupling of the price of oil effective January 1, 1974.

From Algeria we proceeded to Egypt. We stayed over in Cairo briefly. I saw Céline looking down from the balcony of my cousin Mona's apartment in which we were staying. She was fascinated by a trail of wagons each pulled by a donkey. They were stacked with fresh vegetables, fruit and other household needs. Each seller chanted out loud about the quality and low price of whatever he was selling. People devised a simple system to buy from their balconies. They drop a basket dangling from a rope long enough to reach the street level, but tied up at the balcony's railing. Housewives or their maids buy their daily needs from those sellers after a well-known Egyptian trait of bargaining. Upon agreeing, money is to be securely fastened at the bottom of the basket before it is lowered. The seller picks up the money and deposits whatever change remains along with the merchandise. Céline sat on a chair looking down with her head sticking out through the balcony's low-level railing watching with amazement and wide-open eyes.

It was an unforgettable scene when I rushed into the arms of my mother and the rest of family upon arrival at our villa in Victoria, Alexandria. They were all happy to meet my bride. As soon as we all sat in our salon, Céline turned to my mother and told her in perfect Arabic pronunciation what Zakaria taught her back in the United States before we left, *"Hamati sitt tayyebah,"* meaning "my mother-in-law is a kind lady." Every one cracked up laughing while Gamila, the wife of my eldest brother commented that Zakaria had successfully taught Céline *"el-hak lalah."*

My sisters rushed to sew some dresses for Céline when they discovered that her suitcase had been lost en route and offered her what she immediately needed for the night. Céline and I slept in the vacant four-story villa of my brother Mohamed in Roushdy, next door to the villa inhabited by Abdel-Latif El-Baghday, one of the most prominent free officers who joined Gamal Abdel-Nasser's revolution ending Egypt's monarchy in 1952. Our visit was completed by my reunion with an old friend from Minnesota, Galal Aref, and his wife Dody, who gave us a superb cultural tour of Alexandria. Galal is a pediatrician and Dody has a Ph.D. in literature, and they initiated an ongoing annual literary event commemorating Lawrence Durrell, the author of *The Alexandria Quartet*, and his legacy in Alexandria.

One year after our long delayed honeymoon in 1976, President Anwar Sadat summoned me to a meeting with him in Cairo. "As you know, Oweiss (that was the way he used to address me, without a title), we have initiated an open-door policy two years ago. I want you to be the Chief of the Egyptian Economic Mission to the United States with the rank of ambassador. You were highly recommended by our Prime Minister Mamdouh Salem with whom you had met a couple of days ago. With your vast connections, I want you to bring U.S. investments to Egypt." My answer was brief and up to point, "It will be an honor, Mr. President, to undertake such a challenging assignment." We shook hands as he stood up. "Our Chief of the Presidential Cabinet, Hassan Kamel, will work out the details with you." Kamel's letter officially informing me of my appointment conveyed my mission succinctly and left no doubt of its importance. "As you know, Egypt's Open Door policy initiated in 1974 placed the utmost importance on widening and deepening economic ties between Egypt and the Western Countries, in particular the United States," he wrote. "The President is confident that this appointment will enable you to contribute significantly to the establishment of new and stronger dimensions in the economic relationship between the two Countries."

Upon my appointment in 1977 as the Chief of the Egyptian Economic Mission to the United States with rank of ambassador, we relocated to New York. In addition to the staff appointed in Egypt and sent to New York, I hired an outstanding assistant, Cindy Pherson, who had recently graduated from college. Our official residency was at the Sovereign, the high-rise apartment building on East 68th Street and First Avenue. It was a spacious apartment extending from 68th to 69th Streets on the 16th floor. Because of its adequate facilities and spaciousness, there were about fifty ambassadors residing in the building representing their countries at the United Nations. It was not far from the official residency of Kurt Waldheim, Secretary-General of the United Nations, at Sutton Place. From the north side, we could see airplanes landing or taking off from LaGuardia Airport and a continuous flow of cars on the Queensboro Bridge. Almost at the foot of the bridge there was a helipad for helicopters; this was not far from other modes of transportation such as motorcycles, bicycles, and even carts pulled by donkeys, in additions to hundreds of pedestrians on sidewalks, some of whom occasionally stopped for hot dogs, warm pretzels, roasted nuts, or drinks.

While in the first month Céline was preoccupied with the decoration of our residency before we started holding receptions, I started implementing a plan of action to attract investors from the United States. How could I find means of attracting U.S. investments to Egypt other than traditional methods of public speaking and meetings?

I soon devised a successful tactic. I called on David Rockefeller, the chairman of Chase Manhattan Bank. Having studied his personality before our meeting, I played a winning card. He likes to be treated as a head of state. I told him at his office that it would be a pleasure for me to arrange for a special audience with President Sadat in Egypt—if he were to open a branch of Chase Manhattan in Cairo. My plan worked. The meeting took place in Cairo and the bank opened its doors for business. As a result, potential U.S. investors opened accounts at the only American bank in Egypt at the time.

For meetings at the Egyptian Embassy, or at the World Bank, or at the International Monetary Fund in Washington, D.C., I used to shuttle between the two cities. The fare was less than forty dollars. One time in 1977, I was seated next to Ronald Reagan. People then called him "Governor," referring to his last official post as the governor of California. At that time, no one knew that he would be elected president. We had a cordial conversation, especially after I told him about my job. He asked me to convey his respects to President Sadat. He thought very highly of him and described him as "the most courageous leader." At other times, our driver Hussein from Nubia in the southern part of Egypt would drive us between our residence in New York and our home in Kensington. In spite of his young age, he was a cautious driver who never took risks in spite of the congestion in downtown Manhattan and other places.

Before his resignation, President Nixon was warmly greeted by President Sadat who had ordered the preparation of the most beautifully ornamented train of the late King Farouk to travel from Cairo to Alexandria with cheering crowds along the way. Aboard the train, the two presidents agreed to form the Egypt-U.S. Business Council in which top businessmen on both sides would be working together to forge a milestone in the economic relationship between the two countries. The U.S. businessmen included Thomas A. Murphy, Chairman of the Board of General Motors, David C.

Scott, the Chairman of Allis-Chalmers and David Rockefeller, Sr. From the Egyptian side, engineer Niazi Mustafa, an MIT graduate in the 1920s and a highly respectable businessman in the industrial and agricultural sectors, was a great asset. I worked closely with this prominent group and attracted their attention to the need for foreign investments in Egypt. We had periodic meetings in New York, Cairo, and once at Georgetown University.

What helped me in my mission was the image of President Sadat in the United States. With his historic trip to Israel, offering peace in his historic speech before the Israeli Knesset on November 20, 1977, he became a hero to some and an incredibly courageous leader to others. At an official dinner in 1979 given by President Carter in honor of President Sadat, I sat next to Zbigniew Brzezinski, the National Security Advisor to the President. We heard President Carter saying, "I am glad that President Sadat is not an American, because if he were, he would be unbeatable in the forthcoming presidential election in the United States." As it turned out in the final analysis, the sixteen months I spent in New York from August 1977 to the end of December 1978 resulted in a twentyfold increase in U.S. investment in Egypt from what it used to be before I assumed my position in New York. President Sadat conferred upon me the Merit Decoration, First Order, on December 18, 1978.

Ambassador Ghorbal wrote me upon my departure from the diplomatic service that he regretted my leaving. "I know how much university life means to you," he wrote. "Bringing up the young with a high degree of knowledge and responsibility has always been one of your primary objectives. However, let me tell you, on behalf of my country, how much we regret your leaving the Economic and Investment Mission at the Embassy of Egypt. Through the past year and a half, you have given so much of your time, energy, experience, and wisdom to help Egypt, as it seeks to open new vistas for American investors. You have spared no effort to convince many an industry that now is the time to come and invest in our country. Your wide range of relations across the United States, and your many relations in the Arab World, have all been mobilized to this end. We thank you immensely for a job well done."

* * *

Not all of my travels were to Europe and the Middle East. It was early in 1976 when I was contacted by the ambassador of Panama to meet with Dr. Nicolas Ardito Barletta, Panama's Minister of Planning and Economic Policy. He sought my advice on the comprehensive developmental plan his country was embarking on. I accepted the challenge on condition that I visited the country, as I was not familiar with it and did not speak the language. Dr. Barletta had a doctoral degree from the University of Chicago. We hit it off together as we were fellow economists.

In the days I spent in Panama, I gathered information about its resources other than its revenues from the Panama Canal, over which the country did not have full control at that time. Negotiations were ongoing for Panama to assume full control of the 47-mile waterway connecting the Pacific and the Atlantic Oceans. The Panama Canal Authority assumed command over the Canal at noon on December 31, 1999, following the treaty signed between the United States and Panama.

The highlight of my trip was a private meeting with President Omar Torrijos. It was attended by his Minister of Planning. I arranged for a special meeting of Dr. Barletta with Dr. Mohamed Abou Shadi, the Chairman and founder of the Union des Banques Arabes et Françaises, UBAF, as a possible lender of its petrodollars to Panama's development program. At the annual joint meeting of the World Bank and the International Monetary Fund held in 1976 in Manila, Dr. Barletta added me to the Panamanian delegation. It was an opportunity to pursue the implementation of Panama's economic devlopment plan. When President Sadat appointed me ambassador, I discontinued my relationship with Panama as its Senior Economic Advisor.

Upon my return from my post in New York to Georgetown University to resume my teaching and advising duties, I was contacted by Dr. Armand Hammer, an icon in the field of oil exploration, who had discovered oil in Libya. We met at his Washington Liaison office on Pennsylvania Avenue, half a block away from the White House. "In admiration of President Sadat, I wish to explore with him a large investment project for Egypt. It could be mutually beneficial to your country and to my company and its shareholders. I also wish to retain you as a senior economic advisor," he told me. After a handshake, we had several meetings to prepare the groundwork. I got to know a formidable personality.

During a trip together, he told me about his first encounter with the Soviet Union. Upon his graduation from the school of medicine in New York, he decided to visit the land from which his ancestors came before the Bolshevik revolution with a medical gift including an ambulance, medicine and other medical needs. It was early in the 1920s when he landed in Moscow seeking an audience with Lenin. Since he knew of the inadequate facilities in Moscow, he took with him bedsheets and pillows. While impatiently waiting for the appointment, he managed to survive under poor conditions in the best hotel he could find. In order to protect himself against climbing bugs to his bed, he asked for four urns, filled them with water and had each put under one of the legs. Yet he told me that they were clever. They would climb up the wall on their way to the ceiling, position themselves above the bed, and then drop one after the other. We laughed as I discovered his witty sense of humor.

It was related to him that there was a famine in Siberia. Upon enquiring, he found out that the people out there needed about one million bushels of wheat. Being a wealthy American himself, he dispatched a message to his brother Victor in New York to use one million dollars from his account to buy and ship one million bushels of wheat, as the price of a bushel was one dollar at that time. In exchange he got fur of almost an equal value. It was neither a profitable nor a loss-making business deal, but it wiped out the famine prevailing in Siberia at that time. Having heard the story, Lenin asked to see the young American industrialist at once. He told him, "You are the type of businessman I admire." Ever since Armand Hammer had grown familiar with the leaders of the Soviet Union and had an ongoing business with that country.

In the late 1970's I held several meetings with Dr. Hammer and his top management. I convinced them to undertake an immense investment project including extraction of the huge phosphate deposits in the south-west region of the Nile River, ammonia and other by-products industrialization, new roads and urbanization connecting the deposit areas with the Red Sea, in addition to the construction of new port facilities for exports. After having secured a meeting with President Anwar Sadat, we all flew to Cairo in 1980.

The team of Occidental Oil Company had prepared the feasibility study of the 5-billion dollar project and secured the necessary financing from the World Bank, Saudi Arabia, European banks and other donors. Unfortunately, the project was not implemented after President Sadat's assassination on October 6, 1981, because of the inability of President Mubarak to provide the needed leadership.

The proposed project for Egypt involved an investment of over five billion dollars, more than ten times the project of Egypt's Aswan Dam. I advised Dr. Hammer to appoint a respectable businessman as an agent. His selection was Marei Marei, the brother of Sayyed Marei, Egypt's Speaker of the House in the Egyptian Parliament, whose son Hassan was married to President Sadat's daughter. In preparation for the upcoming visit, I went to Egypt to lay the groundwork, met with Sayyed Marei at both his office and his estate close to the pyramids where he had a rare collection of genuine Arabian horses. He asked me to brief him about Hammer. I said, "He is not only a business tycoon but also a great art collector, as well as a well-known philanthropist. Throughout the years, he cultivated a wide network of friends and acquaintances. Once he bragged that he was the only man in history who had been friends with both President Ronald Reagan and Premier Vladimir Lenin." At a meeting with Marei Marei at his home in Zamalek, we talked at length about the immense investment project to be presented to President Anwar Sadat. Unfortunately, he died soon after and his son Hussein took over the business.

We flew to Egypt in two executive jets carrying the senior staff of Occidental Oil Company including the former senator from Tennessee, Albert Gore, Sr., the father of former Vice President Al Gore. Dr. Hammer summoned the whole group at his presidential suite at the Nile Hilton on the eve of the scheduled meeting with President Sadat. It was a lesson in leadership I wish had been recorded. He kept the camera crew accompanying him out of the suite, and orchestrated the meeting as a maestro. He called on those to be involved in the project in a logical manner asking for technical and business briefings. In announcing the end of the meeting by standing up, he named those who will be attending the audience with President Sadat on the following day.

In the limousine taking us to Heliopolis, Armand Hammer

asked me to sit between his wife Frances and him. On the way, for about half an hour, he asked me to rehearse with him as if I were President Sadat. When it was over, he leaned his head on the side and went for a deep sleep for about 20 minutes. Frances whispered so as not to wake him up. "This is the way he reactivates his full energy through sleeping deep for a few minutes," she explained.

After presenting the project, he concluded, "I am in a hurry before I die to do this project for Egypt, because I am now 82 years old."

President Sadat still holding his pipe replied courteously, "Who knows? I may die before you."

His prophecy turned out to be true. President Sadat was killed on October 6, 1981, while Armand Hammer died on December 10, 1990.

Following the meeting and before his departure from Egypt, he decided to travel a long distant to Giza, crossing the crowded metropolitan city of Cairo. His camera crew was instructed to take pictures of Armand Hammer at the pyramids and at the foot of the Sphinx.

President Sadat delegated authority to his Minister of Industry, Taha Zaki. Following the meeting, Taha Zaki asked to visit Occidental plants in the United States. Together with Hussein Marei, they had an informative trip, but Taha Zaki got cold feet because of the immensity of the project and kept procrastinating until after President Sadat died. Taha Zaki looked like a movie star. He was a courteous man but not a doer.

Armand Hammer contacted me to give me the bad news, "I am not used to the way your Minister of Industry is taking us in circles. I decided to call it off. Please inform President Mubarak of my decision with my regrets." Egypt lost one of the single largest investments in its history because of stifling bureaucracy.

Nevertheless, we continued to see one another occasionally, and he frequently called me. Once he called from London. "Remember the Codex Leicester by Leonardo da Vinci you advised me to purchase when you were browsing in the Sotheby's collection in London? I had just bought it at an auction for five million dollars," he told me.

"Congratulations, Dr. Hammer," I exclaimed. "It will remain

an invaluable treasure as it is the original hand-writings and designs of the ingenious painter."

He invited me to attend its showing at the Corcoran Museum across the street from the White House Executive Office Building. It is a collection of the scientific writings written in mirror image. The Codex Leicester later became known as Codex Hammer. As it turned out, it became the most expensive book in history. It was sold at an auction in 1994 to Bill Gates for $30.8 million. At the opening, top personalities were touring with spellbound admiration.

The reason why he chose that particular museum was a story worth mentioning. At his Washington office, Dr. Hammer told me that he had just returned from a visit with Robert Krieger of the Corcoran and related the conversation that he had had.

"I noticed you charge an entrance fee for the visitors of your great art collections," Hammer recounted himself saying.

"Yes, Dr. Hammer," Krieger replied. "We need the money to cover part of our operating expenses."

"How much do you need as an endowment to have the museum open to the public without charge?" Hammer asked.

"One million dollars," replied Krieger.

"You will have it," Hammer replied.

He was a great philanthropist in the arts, education and humanitarian institutions in the United States and elsewhere. In 1982, he founded the United World College at Montezuma in New Mexico to teach international understanding among young students coming from dozens of countries from around the globe with full scholarships. All expenses were paid by the Armand Hammer Foundation. United World College on the West Coast was ranked among the world's top 50 schools for its success in preparing students to enter top American universities.

The last time I shook hands and talked with Armand Hammer was at his 90th birthday in 1988. Céline and I were included in a gala dinner attended by more than two hundred top dignitaries followed by a concert at the Kennedy Center. It was the only time in the world of performing arts that the two of the most famous violinists, Yehudi Menuhin and Isaac Stern, played at the same event. From his lodge, Armand Hammer stood to thank the world-renowned performers and all who had attended. He ended up saying, "We will meet again when I am one hundred." He didn't quite make it, as he died two years later. But I will never forget that, despite the differences among us in age (indeed, he was born four years before my father), and in profession, Armand Hammer and I became close friends in the last decade of his life.

Two weeks after his election, on December 15, 1991, Boutros-Boutros Ghali, the new Secretary-General of the United Nations, wrote to thank me for my tireless efforts to help to elect him. I had managed to have Joseph Reed, the White House Chief of Protocol, to hold a business luncheon with influential personalities at Blair House. I had known Joseph since he was the office director of David Rockefeller, who was chairman of Chase Manhattan Bank when I was ambassador in New York in 1977. Reed felt that President Bush might not be keen to have an Egyptian in that important international post because of his close relationship with the Israeli lobby, and so he first managed to have Dr. Boutros-Boutros Ghali accompany President Sadat in his historical trip to Israel in 1977 with a peace offer. Nevertheless, as we feared U.S. opposition to the nomination, I suggested to Joseph Reed a strategy to have the United States abstain from voting. With U.S. neutrality, the nomination passed in the world body, largely because of many nations around the globe having deep respect for the integrity, brilliance and modesty of the candidate.

I rushed to inform Ambassador Ghorbal. Without hesitation, he contacted influential personalities in the Reagan administration he knew well from the old days at Harvard University in the 1940s. The strategy worked. In the meanwhile, I brought the candidacy of Boutros-Boutros Ghali to the attention of David Abshire, the Chairman of the influential Center for Strategic and International Studies (CSIS) and a former U.S. ambassador to NATO, with whom I had had many intellectual encounters over the years since 1968. He acted quickly and hosted a dinner in honor of Boutros-Boutros Ghali with important policy makers at his home in old town Alexandria, Virginia. Céline and I were engaged in persuasive arguments with the other guests to ensure a successful candidacy.

In 1992, I formed and led a group of Arab-American leaders for a meeting held at the office of Boutros-Boutros Ghali at the United

Nations as a show of our support and solidarity. It was an opportunity to give him a standing proposal I presented to the United Nations concerning a way to assist infant industries in less developed nations. As Secretary-General of the United Nations, we hosted him at Georgetown University in 1993.

The National Bank of Egypt is the largest and oldest banking institution in the entire Middle East. It was established in Cairo on June 25, 1898. Egypt issued a law in 1930 to create the country's central bank to regulate the nation's monetary policy. The National Bank of Egypt functioned as Egypt's Central Bank with all of its supervisory and regulatory functions over all other commercial banks until it was decided to establish a separate institution, the Central Bank of Egypt in the middle of the twentieth century. The National Bank of Egypt has operated as a commercial bank ever since, but its bulletin published by its research department remains an important source of information and statistics about Egypt's economy and its financial sectors.

In the series of the Distinguished National Bank of Egypt Commemorative Lecture Program, I was asked to present my research on the phenomenon of the underground economy. In my study entitled "The Underground Economy with Special Reference to the Case of Egypt," I estimated that it is even larger than Egypt's officially reported GDP. Mahmoud Abdel-Aziz, the Chairman of the National Bank of Egypt, introduced me on December 19, 1994 at the large auditorium of the National Bank of Egypt in its high-rise newly constructed headquarters facing west on the Nile River. Among the large crowd there were ministers of the Egyptian cabinet including Fouad Hussein, dignitaries such as former ambassador Ashraf Ghorbal, and my former colleague the architect of Egypt's open-door policy Sherif Lotfy, prominent businessmen, policy makers, media and others.

Following my introduction of the phenomenon that had been described by at least sixteen different names such as the parallel economy, the hidden economy, the off-books economy, the subterranean economy, the self-service economy, the border economy, and others, I showed that is to be found in every country in varying degrees. The reasons for the existence of an underground economy are many but they include tax evasion and concealment of illegal activities. Unlike other attempts to estimate its size mainly by notable economists from Latin America, I applied macroeconomic theory of saving function to estimate the extent of Egypt's underground economy. The National Bank of Egypt published the study.

It was customary to give the speaker and spouse either a one-week tour of Luxor and Aswan to see ancient Egyptian monuments on a Nile cruise, or to go to a sea resorts on the Red Sea and visit Mount Sinai. Since we did the former tour twice already, we chose the latter and brought along our children at our expense. While in Cairo, we stayed at the Marriott Hotel in Zamalek on the west side of the Nile River. The hotel was constructed on the northern side of the palace originally built by Khedive Ismail, the ruler of Egypt, to host Queen Victoria and Queen Eugenie of France, the wife of Napoleon III, on the occasion of the celebrations for the opening of the Suez Canal. The ruler of Egypt was charmed by the French Queen's noted beauty, charm and great extravagance. In one of the large high-ceiling reception halls with artistically decorated walls, a large painting of Queen Eugenie was hanging. As part of the celebrations, a Khedivial Opera House in Cairo was built where the opera *Aida* was first performed on December 24, 1871. Giuseppe Verdi was commissioned by Egypt to compose it. We flew to Horgada on the Red Sea, a beautiful resort, before we flew to Sharm-el-Sheikh, where we can never forget how delicious the seafood was. We were then driven to Ras Mohamed and other resorts on the Red Sea until we reached Taba, the northernmost location in Egypt looking at the Israeli border and across the Gulf of Aqaba, where we could see the city of Aqaba in Jordan. We were also driven to the middle of the Sinai desert and stayed at the third-century St. Catherine's Monastery. At its side there is an old wooden box that can be cranked up by a rope after identifying the incoming person. It was an old method that gave rise to the idea of an elevator. The ancient monastery was built in a valley looking up to two gigantic mountains, Mount Moses and Mount St. Catherine. Next to the monastery, there is a bush that the monks believe was the burning tree at which God spoke to Moses. We climbed up uneven rocks, where we had to carefully jump from one level to another, with the help of a Bedouin guide that we had hired to show us the best route up. It took us approximately five hours to reach the top of Mount St. Catherine. We were amazed to see a small church and a tiny mosque at the top. No one knows when monks carried up there stone by stone to build a small church while devout Muslims later on did the same monumental effort to build a small mosque. It was believed that a young girl by the name of Catherine, from a Roman family, was slain in Alexandria, Egypt, by her own relatives after they found out that she became a Christian. One century later, she appeared in a dream to one of the monks, asking him to bring her head to the top of the mountain that was hundreds of miles away from Alexandria, and add her scull to a heap of sculls at the Monastery which can still be visited today. She was later canonized by the Pope and became known as St. Catherine. Throughout history, St. Catherine's Monastery was given unique gifts in gold and silver particularly from Czarist Russia. It houses original scrolls and manuscripts.

I had other occasions to speak in Egypt, the largest of which was on October 12, 2003. In preparation for the event, Mohammed Nosseir, an envoy from the Egyptian-American Friendship Society, headed by Dr. Ibrahim Fawzi, a former minister of industry and the General Authority for Investments and Free Zones, flew in to meet with me in Washington. Over lunch at the Cosmos Club, the politically active and concerned Egyptian extended the formal invitation to speak in Cairo on "Egyptian-American Relations." The event was held at Cairo's Grand Hyatt main ballroom. It was attended by a large number of dignitaries. Mary Ott, a diplomat at the U.S. Embassy in Cairo, rushed to see me after the event. "Do you remember me? I was your student at Georgetown University." The event was widely published in the country's media. The journalist Adel Hammouda published a long article in *Al-Ahram* headlined "Thank you, Dr. Oweiss."

In his usual talk at the late afternoon lunch, which was the main meal in Egypt, my father used the gathering and attention of our family to speak on the issue of the day or on any other relevant matter, be it family, neighborhood, schooling, national or international subjects. When I was about six, he explained the human tragedy of the Jews in Germany and the ugly side of racism. At school, I asked a favorite teacher to allocate some time to discuss the issue. Three years later, during World War II, I formed a club called "Jewish Plight." Its purpose was to help our Egyptian Jews in case Hitler's army occupied Egypt by appealing to the families of my fellow students to help hide them. It was a naïve idea, but it reflected the humanitarian sentiments of people throughout the Islamic civilization to provide the Jews amongst them with full protection and security at a time when they were persecuted in Christian European societies.

Ever since I was a young boy, I thought it was my duty to be politically active against Nazism and the continuation of British occupation of Egypt. Whenever there was a call for community service, I found myself to be in the forefront of volunteers. As I grew up, the issues of activism I became involved with became multiple and diversified. I was a teenager when an alien ideology was implanted in the Middle East under the banner of Zionism. As it turned out, it divided the peoples of the region into two opposing groups: Jews and Arabs. Ever since 1948, there had been devastating wars while peace has become a far-fetched dream. Following the continuation of the Middle East tension often erupting in wars, I have been a commentator and an activist for the Palestinian inalienable rights of self determination and an end to Israeli occupation, according to the United Nations resolution to enforce peace as the only rational alternative to ensure safety for all and to safeguard U.S. interests as well.

Since before the creation of Israel in 1948 until the present day, all presidents of the United States have had the Arab-Israeli conflict on their agendas. Yet, with the exception of President Eisenhower, all other presidents supported Israel right or wrong, providing it with not only billions of dollars in aid but also with the most sophisticated and destructive weapons, to ensure that it had a definite advantage over its combined Arab neighbors even if it violated the terms under which those weapons were provided, including the use against civilians, and protecting it with the American veto in the United Nations. And there has been a continuous mobilization through Western media for the support of a Jewish state after the Holocaust in which millions were brutally killed or gassed to death.

There has also been a campaign of silencing any voice criticizing the Israeli Zionist state by using the whip of anti-Semitism, even if it comes from the Jews themselves such as Noam Chomsky, Israel Shahak, Jonathan Ben Artzi and many other fair-minded Israeli citizens, as well as Jews elsewhere seeking peaceful coexistence. Zionism turns out to be a form of racism, as shown factually in statements by Fayez A. Sayegh on October 17, 1975, and on November 10, 1975. The United Nations General Assembly Resolution 3379, which claimed to "determine that Zionism is a form of racism and racial discrimination," was adopted on November 10, 1975, by a vote of 72 to 35 (with 32 abstentions). Yet, for political reasons, it was revoked sixteen years later under the auspices of the United States administration by Resolution 46/86 on December 16, 1991, on the pretext that such action could help move the Middle East peace process forward. Nevertheless, the facts on the ground have revealed that indeed Zionism is a form of racism and racial discrimination while peace has not been attainable simply because Israel under Zionism does not want it.

With its expansionary policy, Israel under Zionism has been at war almost continuously ever since it was established in 1948. Its program of confiscating Arab land in occupied territories to build Jewish settlements is against all rules of international conventions and in defiance of United Nations resolutions—even its strongest ally and protector the United States considers settlements to be illegal and an obstacle to peace. Such a program can be described as armed theft creating furor and anger which add further dangerous instability in the Middle East. Its war against Gaza using phosphoric bombs against civilians in defiance of the rules and regulations of the United States that supplies Israel with such weapons of mass destruction, and its seizure of the entire population of Gaza must lead to an application of Newton-Oweiss Law. Israel under Zionism keeps its iron-fist policy against the Palestinians, bulldozing homes of those resisting occupation and denying them their inalienable rights to self-determination. Such intolerable conditions cannot be sustained. The only rational way out to save Israel in spite of itself is peace and an end to occupation so that Jews and Palestinians, both Christian and Muslim Arabs, can live in peace as they did throughout history when Jews were persecuted in western Christian nations. Otherwise, Israel under Zionism is bound to self-destruction sometime in the future.

During my last semester of teaching at Georgetown main campus, I was shocked along with all people around the globe by the attack on the United States and the death of thousands of innocent human beings. My daughter Yasmeen, then working in New York City and living not far from the World Trade Center towers, called to tell us that a plane had hit one of the towers. My wife and I turned on the television and saw the smoke from the tower, and then we saw the second tower being hit. It was heartbreaking to witness some people throwing themselves from high. We also saw the two towers collapse. Two former students of mine were among the victims of the attack in New York and a colleague of mine with her husband and children were killed in one of the hijacked planes. When I met my two classes on the very same day, I was too depressed to teach, but I instilled in their minds and hearts the courage to overcome the ordeal.

When I realized later that it was a premeditated attack on the United States, I could see the writing on the wall of those who wished to use the tragedy to create a further chasm with the Muslim world. Sympathy towards the United States was overwhelmingly noticeable in the furthest corners of the globe. It was an opportunity for the United States to build upon world support in the best interest of mankind. The people of the United States as well as of many countries supported a war to punish those responsible for the tragedy of September 11, 2001. Yet the Bush Administration blew it when it decided to wage war in 2003 against Iraq in violation of international law. President Bush kept saying that Saddam Hussein was lying about his possession of weapons of mass destruction. History now shows that indeed one of them was lying.

On September 11, 2001, the Council on Egyptian-American Relations released the following statement:

Statement from the Council on Egyptian-American Relations
By Ibrahim M. Oweiss
September 11, 2001

The Council on Egyptian-American Relations is terribly shocked and extremely dismayed with utter disbelief for today's attack on and demolition of the World Trade Center as well as parts of the Pentagon. We deplore in the strongest possible manner such terror that may claim in the final analysis the lives of thousands of innocent people on the ground, in buildings or in the crashed planes, and the many who were injured, maimed or otherwise affected directly or indirectly.

Tragedy should make us come close together and help us to absorb the deep pain and go forward in life with reflection, understanding, and compassion towards one another. It is not the time to rush to accusations of anyone without real proof or concrete evidence. We stand by fairness and justice. Those who were behind the planning and execution of such unprecedented tragedy should be brought to world trial. A proof of the charges against those being implicated should be presented without generalizations to religions, ethnicities, or countries of origin. Stereotyping should be avoided at these crucial moments our nation and the world are going through. It is enough pain and suffering of the many innocent people that lost their beloved ones. There is no need to create further unjustifiable and unfounded accusation against other innocent ones who could suffer for no reason other than cruel generalizations. We appeal to rationalism rather than emotionalism in helping us overcome the scar deeply felt in our hearts and souls.

The Council on Egyptian-American Relations believes in our strong character of endurance and in the great and positive spirit of our nation with fairness and justice for all.

The tragedy of September 11, 2001, was used to widen the chasm between the United States on the one hand and the Muslims and the Arabs on the other hand. The Zionist-manipulated media together with southern evangelists joined forces to create an enemy image of the Muslims and the Arabs. After 9/11, I felt a different treatment for the first time since I set foot on the soil of the United States. While I was about boarding a flight from Washington, D.C. in January 2002, I was asked to go for another security check.

"Why are you singling me out?" I asked.

"You do not ask questions, just follow me," said one of the security agents.

After thoroughly searching a seventy-year-old gentleman, the same guard accompanied me to the plane, but told me in a rather embarrassed voice, "You were singled out because your middle name is Mohamed." I despised the venom of bigotry and the ugly, unjustifiable discrimination I was exposed to. Following a meeting at the Council on Egyptian-American Relations, I issued the following statement in an attempt to build on positives rather than leave us being dragged into the blind road of negatives:

February 6, 2002
Statement of mission
Misunderstanding Islam became apparent after the tragedy of September 11.

The Council on Egyptian-American Relations issued a strong message on September 11 denouncing the criminal attack on the U.S.A. and called for bringing those responsible to world trial.

The image of Egypt and the Arabs has been distorted in the U.S.A. and Europe especially after September 11.

Good relations between the U.S.A., on the one hand, and Egypt and the Arabs on the other hand, is not only essential for the best interests of both sides, their people, and governments, but also for their interdependency and mutual cord of security and stability.

It is important to reach out to the people of the United States through culture and continuous flow of exchanges of scholars, academicians, writers, reporters, policymakers, and trade missions.

The Council on Egyptian-American Relations in collaboration with George Mason University is interested in the production of "The Last Pharaoh" depicting the revelation of the oneness of God and "Shahadut Alla Elah Illa Allah" to be prominently and respectfully shown on the stage, on a movie, and on tapes.

"Nathan the Wise" with its message "Salah-el Din El-Ayoubi on the U.S. stage, with the three religions, Judaism, Christianity, and Islam believing in one God" has already been produced in the same manner and is having a great impact on the minds and hearts of the viewers.

Production of such plays at the highest professional level will pave the way for their appearances on Broadway, and a movie based on the play can be vastly effective.

To secure the above goals and others it is important to finance this non-governmental organization.

It is also important to have funds available for a building, staff and effective operations of the Council on Egyptian-American Relations.

Funds should also be secured to pay for visiting scholars from the Arab world. Their impact on educational and cultural spheres in the U.S. will undoubtedly help reversing the distorted image of Arabs in general and Egypt, Saudi Arabia and the UAE in particular.

I became an activist in this regard through my public speeches, television and radio interviews, public debates, writings and donations. With other concerned Americans, I joined the efforts of former President Jimmy Carter, former President Bill Clinton, Walter Cronkite and others to give hope for a better future by attempting to contain the harm done under George W. Bush and to reverse it. In his circular letter to all those concerned, the icon of U.S. television, broadcaster Walter Cronkite, wrote:

When I anchored the evening news, I kept my opinions to myself. But now, more than ever, I feel I must speak out. That's because I am deeply disturbed by the dangerous and growing influence of people like Pat Robertson and Jerry Falwell on our nation's political leaders. Over the years, Robertson and Falwell have gained considerable influence on local school boards, in the administration and in Congress. They have shrewdly twisted the traditional healing role of religion into an intolerant political platform. The Religious Right's influence over America's politicians has gone too far. Please join me in offering a voice of tolerance, civility and true compassion in the political process by supporting The Interfaith Alliance's mission.

Both Céline and I not only joined Walter Cronkite's efforts but also donated money and spared no effort to continue our support of his mission both in word and in action even after his death on July 17, 2009, at age 93.

On September 10, 2002, I was invited with some Arab-American leaders to meet with President George W. Bush. At the meeting I stated, with due respect to whatever decision he would soon make, "In waging a war against Iraq, you would win easily, but you will never ever win the peace." It seemed to me that the president did not really understand the extent of what the military can do. Yet he came up with a good statement denouncing bigotry.

But it had little effect. After Daniel Pipes translated a letter to the editor published in Arabic in one of the Egyptian newspapers, under the provocative title "Cannibals," on August 28, 2003, I was contacted by Fox News to comment on it. The Egyptian letter writer had been disgusted at the release of pictures of the bodies of Saddam Hussein's two sons after being gunned down. Unfortunately, she made an ugly generalization in describing Americans as cannibals. Instead of interviewing me, O'Reilly started a repulsive attack on all Egyptians and on President Mubarak for having "allowed its publication." I refused his illogical claims and blamed Daniel Pipes for translating what I called "trash" and the *Wall Street Journal* for allowing its publication. To demonstrate the ugly side of bigotry, I will provide below a postcard I received after the interview with the *O'Reilly Factor* on Fox, and a letter I wrote to President George W. Bush.

> We watched you on the O'Reilly program spouting like a barking dog—full of crap—you are a phony lying muslim terrorist & should be kicked out of U S A & sent back to your 5ᵗʰ rate egypt or wherever you came from. And your koran is a sack of garbage filled with lies and fairy tales—a disgrace to Christ Our Lord—you don't deserve to live here in freedom & eat our good Christian food. So drop dead & burn in hell you old sack of shit—see?
> Patrick F. X. McNernery
> A Catholic War Veteran

I did not respond to the gentleman, but wrote a letter to President Bush.

Dear President Bush,

Your words at our meeting on September 10, 2002, have had a profound echo in all of our hearts when you said:

"Bigotry is not part of our soul." "In order for us to reject the evil done to America on September 11th, we must reject bigotry in all its forms." "We treasure our friendship with Muslims and Arabs around the world."

Regrettably, I received the enclosed postcard allegedly typewritten by one who claims to be in admiration of you. As a Republican, I gave my vote to you to lead all of us, proud Americans, and to lead the world based on the great heritage and principles of our nation. Your statements above are quite admirable, yet to hear views such as those expressed on the enclosed postcard is divisive and quite disturbing.

I am proud to have taught at the top universities such as Georgetown University, Harvard University, The Johns Hopkins University, and the University of Minnesota for forty years with thousands of appreciative students under me. My contributions to higher learning education were recognized at the highest level by your thoughtful letter to me on January 24, 2002. Nevertheless, to get insults advocating bigotry from someone who claims to be your admirer is a contradiction in terms.

I do not wish to take your time from your great responsibilities. Yet, I believe that you ought to know that there are destructive negative views that are alarming.

Respectfully yours,
Ibrahim M. Oweiss

At the end of March 2003, I had a sharp and unbearable pain in my stomach. I thought I was going to die. Having noticed a silent pain on my face on his way out to have dinner with some friends, I saw anxiety in the eyes of my son Kareem, who was almost 23 then.

I told him:

Life is for the living with all its ups and downs, its challenges and rewards as well as its disappointments.

A rose smiles with beauty before it fades away.
Grieve less upon the loss of the beloved
But let their good deeds be eternally alive in your mind.

I called two physicians: James Foster, our superb family doctor, and Ashraf El-Khodary, a great friend of mine since I came to Washington, D.C. in 1967. Upon consultations with one another, Dr. Foster made the arrangements for me to be admitted to Georgetown University Hospital on March 31, 2003. My wife drove me to the hospital's emergency room, as I did not want to disturb our neighbors if an ambulance were called. I was given tranquilizers but it was a long waiting time amongst screams and the hustle and bustle of doctors, nurses, residents and medical students coming and going until early on the following day when a room became available, I was rolled in and put in bed, surrounded by my wife, my son and his new bride Julia (Julie) Noble White. My daughter Yasmeen was working in New York and could not be with us on time following the sudden sharp pain I had had. While I was rolled in the Emergency Room, Julie held my hand and kissed it. I was moved as thought it might be the end of my life. As she leaned down, I kissed her and said, "Take care of Kareem for the rest of your life because I know how much you love one another." I saw tears forming above her lower eyelids.

The final diagnosis was pancreatitis. Some tiny stones were detected that needed to be removed. Thank God, a surgery was not performed. Instead a specialist from George Washington University Hospital, Dr. Eriani, used a laser method to crush them without the mess of an operation, avoiding a long recovery period. It was a quick stay in the hospital with successful results, after which I resumed my normal activities.

Ten days later, Jim Brown, a vice president of Pratt and Whitney, asked me to arrange for high-level meetings in Qatar for George David, the Chairman of the Board of General Dynamics of which Pratt and Whiney was one of its subsidiaries. I flew to Qatar, and as soon as I met George David at Doha's Airport flying on the company's jet, he bombarded me with questions about Qatar and the regional Gulf countries he was then touring. It was the first and last time I saw him. He struck me as an astute, quick-minded business leader but unemotional. He certainly lacked the warm, friendly attitude I value with the top leaders I encounter. I arranged for a meeting for him with Ahmed Bin Abdullah Al-Mahmoud who was a former student of mine at Georgetown University. He had then assumed the position of Qatar's Minister of State for Foreign Affairs and was a Member of the Ministers Council after having served his country as ambassador to the United States.

On my way back, at Dulles airport I was approaching an immigration booth to have my passport stamped, when an official attendant shouted at me, "Stop in your place. Do not move, do not come close" — as if I had the plague or carried a weapon of mass destruction. He asked me to follow him but to keep a distance behind him. I obeyed but I was bewildered, not fearful, at a situation that I had never been exposed to in my lifetime of traveling. His supervisor rushed me to a special booth.

"Did you have a recent treatment at a hospital?" Then he added, "You look distinguished. Besides I saw you on television on NBC and CNN when you were invited to help explain some questions pertaining to oil prices and developments in the Middle East."

I was partially relieved. After I informed the supervisor, surrounded by detectives and an armed policeman, the procedure I recently had at Georgetown University Hospital, he said, "Radiation was detected in your body as you were approaching one of our booths. I had the same procedure myself and that is why I thought it may be an explanation of what was detected in your body." I was relieved to hear his words, but disheartened to think of what their initial suspicion must have been.

The aftermath of 9/11 was disastrous for the United States because of George W. Bush's lack of vision. He flexed his muscles and relied on the military not knowing that there is a limit to what the military can do. Following the terror attacks, the overwhelming sentiments of the people around the globe were for the United States. President Bush did not capture that opportunity to build on the goodwill that had prevailed around the globe. Instead of using the world community and its institutions such as the United Nations, in addition to bilateral and multilateral relations with other governments and peoples, he came up with his policy, "He who is not with me is against me," opposite to the visionary policy of Winston Churchill during World War II, "He who is not against me is with me." President George W. Bush kept repeating the word "terrorism" and all of its derivatives rather than using such descriptive term as "international crimes" that can be translated into the basis for joint action under the auspices of the United Nations. With time, the word became hollow and devoid of any meaning. Instead of using a conciliatory phraseology, he opted to call his adversaries the "axis of evil," evoking Germany and its allies during World War II.

Another axis comprising the neocons, the southern Baptist evangelists, the Zionist lobby, Fox News and others, manipulated the Bush administration. They succeeded in helping George W. Bush win a second term in November 2004, no matter how narrow the election results were. He had in fact lost the popular vote in 2000, after all. The two most influential individuals swaying him to wage the internationally illegal war against Iraq were two Zionists, Richard Pearl and Paul Wolfowitz. The fabrication of intelligence about Saddam Hussein's weapons of mass destruction, the most single important factor that made our legislators vote for the internationally illegal war on Iraq, will continue to stain Bush's presidency.

In his last tour of the Arabian Gulf as President of the United States, in December 2008, President Bush was shown disrespect towards him in at least two instances, while he was facing the lowest poll rating inside a country in which he became known as the worst president in the history of the United States, as former President Jimmy Carter and senior White House correspondent Helen Thomas called him. The first incident was when Sheikh Sultan Ben Zayed Al-Nahiyan, a highly respected and prominent member of the ruling family of the United Arab Republic, refused to shake hands with President Bush. In many circles, I heard nothing but high praise for Sheikh Sultan who expressed the Arab feelings towards President Bush in a dignified manner. The second was when an angry journalist hurled two shoes at him and called him "dog" at joint press conference with Nouri al-Maliki, the Iraqi Prime Minister, in Baghdad's Green Zone on December 13, 2008. "This is a good-bye kiss from the Iraqi people, dog," shouted the journalist, Muntazer al-Zaidi. In the Arab culture, hitting someone with a shoe is a grave insult, while dogs are considered unclean. The attack highlighted the contempt felt by the Arab masses. I have no doubt that the shoes thrown in disgust to President Bush could be auctioned for millions of dollars.

Using the pretext that the country was in danger and was at war, following 9/11 and the subsequent invasion of Afghanistan, President Bush ordered the opening of the Guantanamo Bay detention camp in the southern part of Cuba for captured prisoners considered by the U.S. adminstration as "enemy combatants." They were not brought to trial; rather, they were tortured and inhumanly mistreated in violation of intrernational law and international treaties concerning prisoners of war. Needless to say, such treatments were in violation of the great principles embodied in the Constitution and the solid foundations upon which the country was built. To get around accusations of detention without trial, the U.S. government chose a non-U.S. territory to open the detention camp.

Following 9/11, George W. Bush had swiftly passed his Patriot Act to give the presidency more power and to subject United States citizens to what would have been otherwise regarded as illegal arrests and unlimited detentions without trial. The American Civil Liberties Union and other liberal institutions, think tanks, institutions of higher learning, and individuals, including prominent well-known personalities, carried the banner of opposition to such fascist tactics. An outcome of the enactment of the Patriot Act by a democracy such as the United States is to give an excuse to other countries to expand their authority in police states. A good example was the case of Egypt. Following President Sadat's assassination on October 6, 1981, the Egyptian government applied an Emergency Law, which has been in effect ever since. After years of the government promising to end the country's state of emergency, Parliament, in May 2010, approved a government request to extend it for two years. Thus official authorities kept their right to arrest people without charge, detain prisoners indefinitely, limit freedom of expression and assembly, and maintain a special security court. Demonstrators in the country poured out in the streets, carrying banners of *Kefaya*, meaning "enough" and calling for an end of the emergency law. An apologist for the government argued that since the Patriot Act is still in force in the U.S., Egypt did not have to rescind the law.

Nevertheless, as a believer in the resiliency and resourcefulness of the American people, through their democracy, educational institutions, think tanks, non-governmental organizations, civil society, and the system of checks and balances, I know a correction is bound to happen. After all, McCarthyism did not last after its initiator Senator Joseph McCarthy was opposed by similar groups in the 1950s. By the same token, it was no wonder that President Obama right after his inauguration announced his intention to close the Guantanamo Bay detention camp.

5

Concluding Words

Throughout my life, I learned neither to lose hope nor ever to burn bridges. Hope is the light that can always guide us to the future, no matter how dimmed it may become at certain moments or even if one is being engulfed by total darkness. In such moments, create your own light in your mind through your belief in Almighty God, the ultimate rescuer. Through your will to overcome, cells of new hope and new light may be created and multiplied.

Burning bridges, on the other hand, is not compatible with co-existence. One can never imagine that a hand from a distant past may come along one day to pull you out from whatever abyss you had fallen into. I look forward to continue my role in life with rigor and hope.

If an unexpected event occurs to me such as a car accident, I never lose my temper but rather face the situation in the cool manner that is typical of me. I get out of the vehicle and ask about the other driver who ran a red light. I may even write a poem describing the accident, as the one shown on page 117 above, which serves me as an outlet with a sense of humor. When a hurricane erupts with tremendous power leaving human beings utterly helpless, and if I suffer from its consequences such as delaying my travel plans, I accept it with tranquil resignation. I resort to reading, writing or otherwise talking about it as I follow its development. At the end of August 2011, my wife and I planned to return from our vacation condominium in Madeira Beech, on an Island in Western Florida in the Gulf of Mexico, with a breathless view of the sunset and a wide sand beach as white as snow. A huge storm called Irene erupted. While watching from our balcony its strong wind and the formation of its mighty dark clouds and pouring rain, I wrote the following:

Irene

A ferocious girl named Irene
became furious when insulted by Arlene
Madly turning around the pupil of one eye
But moving quickly before saying goodbye
She smashes windows and tears down doors
She whistles twists, rumbles and snores
She unleashes galloping winds here and there
Pouring its wrath with buckets of rain everywhere
Downing wires, flooding areas among falling trees
What mess she is leaving behind? What debris?
Go away, no one will ever marry you, none will say hi
With your anger, temperament, and one eye
Good-bye good-bye good-bye.

Madeira Beach, Florida on August 27, 2011

Throughout my life, including travel in all continents except Australia, I have always searched for the good in the human beings I met to build upon it a meaningful relationship.

Religions can play a positive role in advancing the good in human beings provided that they are not used to separate people of different religions. When a group of religious zealots wages a war against people of another religion advocating "God is on our side," I find that the claim defies logic. I am a believer in one God, the creator of all, so why would He favor one group over another? Moses, Jesus, Muhammad and others were all messengers from the One God.

Cultures may instill values of self-discipline in people's minds and hearts such as the Tokugawa tradition of law and order and neo-Confucianism as practiced in Japan and in the Far East. Nevertheless, what works is a structure of four distinct classes, the warriors, the farmers, the artisans and the merchants in a solidly woven cultural fabric with dignity, respect and self-devotion.

Philosophers can have a significant effect on certain societies. In my early youth, I observed how Mao Zedong was able to convince millions in China of his teachings, which became known as Maoism, the ideology of the Communist Party of China. Even though I have always been an anti-communist, I must admit that Mao's impact on his people was remarkable. He laid the groundwork for the remarkable growth of China ever since the 1950s.

Being a firm believer in, and an advocate of, the idea that there is no monopoly over truth, I have always had an open mind when listening to others. I benefit from exchange of ideas no matter how old I get and no matter where I am.

I firmly believe in respecting the dignity of all people and each human being. At the end of one of my classes on the first day in the fall semester of 1997, a student, David Griffith Ross, came to greet me and inform me that I taught his father, John B. Ross, who had graduated from Georgetown University in 1970. David's father had urged him to take my course. At a luncheon meeting with John after the semester was over, he asked me, "What can a group of your former students do for you upon retirement in five years from now?"

"The establishment of a program of Human Dignity Studies at Georgetown University," I replied. "I think it is bigger in scope than 'Human Rights' and hence the latter can be part of it.

"And possibly an 'Ibrahim M. Oweiss Chair of Islamic Economic Thought,'" he suggested.

He started the process of raising the necessary funds for the project, but it was never completed for one reason or another. Maybe a reader of this book on whom I have left an impact will some day restart the process. It would be the best tribute to the ideas I believe in.

Yvonne Minchella, a British Airways hostess, asked for my advice concerning her own 8-year-old son, William, from the heart of a devoted mother. Without hesitation, I said it is important to give William unlimited doses of love by continuously expressing her feelings verbally and in action. In addition, she should be speaking with him rather than talking at him. The best investment parents can do for their children is in good education no matter how much the cost may be.

At the beginning of my memoirs, I wrote a page of advice to my children and students. I am ending the book with my view on supreme greatness:

With these words I wrote and read to my last class in May 2009, I ended 48 years of teaching in institutions of higher learning in the United States. I was inspired by Sheikha Mozah bint Nasser Al-Misned for her devotion to humanity and excellence in education.

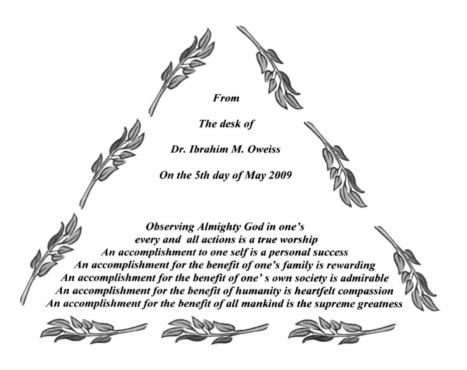

From

The desk of

Dr. Ibrahim M. Oweiss

On the 5th day of May 2009

Observing Almighty God in one's
every and all actions is a true worship
An accomplishment to one self is a personal success
An accomplishment for the benefit of one's family is rewarding
An accomplishment for the benefit of one's own society is admirable
An accomplishment for the benefit of humanity is heartfelt compassion
An accomplishment for the benefit of all mankind is the supreme greatness

CPSIA information can be obtained at www.ICGtesting.com
Printed in the USA
BVOW071123100213

312797BV00001B/1/P